FREEDOM SEEKER

Revised Edition

Tiffani Harvey

Written Words Publishing LLC
14189 E Dickinson Drive, Unit F
Aurora, Colorado 80014
www.writtenwordspublishing.com

Freedom Seeker © 2015 by Tiffani Harvey
Revised Edition

All rights reserved. No part of this publication may be reproduced, stored in a retrieval system, or transmitted in any form by any means, electronic, mechanical, photocopying, recording, or otherwise, without the prior permission of the author.

Published by Written Words Publishing LLC 9/16/2020

ISBN: 978-1-7332357-4-7 (paperback)
ISBN: 978-1-7332357-5-4 (eBook)

Library of Congress Control Number: 2020915069

Cover Designed by Written Words Publishing LLC

Manufactured and printed in the United States of America

Reviews

"Suggestions in Freedom Seeker are good suggestions for EVERYONE." Ken R.

"I wish every girl in high school could read these books. Women in shelters should read them. What a difference that would make!" Ellen

"Tiffani Harvey...has an innate strength driving her to question the automatic assumptions of authority which diminished her innate quest for independence and self-reliance in the name of 'protecting' herself from perceived threats... With grace, compassion, experience and solid practical advice...Tiffani reaches out to empower others by helping them to identify and answer the necessary questions and challenges at every stage of their walk to freedom, by casting a light on her own struggle while empowering individuals and the people who love and care for them with remarkable insight that can only arise from meeting personal challenges head on and succeeding!" A. R. Koheen

Table of Contents

Foreword viii

Acknowledgements ix

Chapter 1: Practical Living: How to Make Everyday Choices (and Stick to Your Choices) 1

    Introduction 1

    Be Safe 2

Chapter 2: Practical Living: How to Choose 4

    Childhood 4

    Family Life 5

    My Grandparents 6

    Church Background 8

    School 8

Chapter 3: Taking Medication and Choosing Doctors 11

Chapter 4: Making Choices by Setting Boundaries 18

    Lifestyle Choices 19

    Religion 20

    Smoking and Vaping 21

    Alcohol 29

    Illegal Drugs 41

Chapter 5: Learning How to Budget Your Money 47

    Handling Your Money 49

    Saving Money 50

    Credit Cards 51

    Gambling 52

    Lending Money to Friends 52

  Borrowing Money 53

  Giving Money to People 54

Chapter 6: Local Transportation 58

  Disability Van 58

  Riding the City Bus 59

  Driving 62

Chapter 7: Learning a Job or a Career 65

  School or College 65

  My College Choices 66

Chapter 8: Employment 70

  Don't Be Afraid to Make a Mistake! 72

  Gaining More Independence 75

Chapter 9: The Challenges of Living on Your Own 76

Chapter 10: Contact People 87

  Making Friends 88

Chapter 11: Boundaries for Dating 92

Chapter 12: Keeping Yourself Safe 95

Chapter 13: Dating and Marriage: Protecting Yourself from Sexual Harassment 107

Chapter 14: Children 118

Chapter 15: Long Distance Traveling 134

Chapter 16: Protecting Yourself in General 148

  Unsafe Behaviors 153

Chapter 17: Money Wise 157

Chapter 18: Car Safety Tips 160

Chapter 19: Resources in the Community 161

Chapter 20: Is Guardianship Good or Bad and Do You Need or Want One? 168
   Guardianship and Intellectually Disabled Individuals 181
   Understanding Guardianship 181
Chapter 21: Where My Strength Lies 183
About the Author 194

Foreword

The reason for this book is to help people who want to make their own choices. The author writes about her own mistakes so readers can avoid making the same mistakes. She wants you to learn *how to* make your own choices. This book is meant to help others know what kind of questions they should ask before making choices. This book is written for:

People who have MH and Intellectual Disabilities

Family Members and
Professionals of People with Disabilities

Middle School and High School Students

Teachers and Counselors

Survivors of Violence

She wants to help people learn to ask questions and get answers before making big choices.

She wants to help people get as much independence as their health will allow.

She wants to help everyone save money and buy only what they can afford!

She asks you to read and understand everything you are asked to sign.

Acknowledgements

I need to start by thanking Mariaelena Wareham and her staff. It is from my experiences of watching them with their clients that I felt the need to write my story.

Next, I want to thank my parents, especially my mom, Judy Singer. She helped me remember a lot of what I wanted to share. We spent many hours on the phone, and she spent many hours proofreading my work! Thank you, Mom!

Then there's Eli Harvey. Eli started off as my prayer partner and neighbor who lived across the street. Eli has seen me through the best and worst of times. *He's still here! He's wonderful! I will love him always!*

I want to thank my good friends, Randall Luce and Carol Marie, who have been here for me from the beginning.

I want to thank the late Cheryl Corkrum and Terry Orr who prayed for me from the very beginning.

I want to thank all of my proofreaders over the years. They include: The late Allan Orr, Janet Coleman, Linda Noble, Jennifer Huseland, and Holly and Paul Hyndman.

(If you know someone who proofed this book and was not listed, let me know so I can add their name to the list. Thank you.)

I want to thank Pastor John and Sandy Repsold and Pastor Neil and Carol Anderson for their spiritual help the last 6-7 years of this journey.

I'd like to thank Ted Medina for helping me on the computer and going beyond job requirements to help me.

I want to thank Lance Morehouse for helping me emotionally when the "system" would anger me so badly and he would help calm me down.

I would like to thank the seven people who took the time to be interviewed. These people wish to remain nameless.

I want to thank Sue Eller who introduced me to Smashwords.

I want to thank Leona Gow for the many times she has saved me time and money.

Finally, I want to thank the Author of Life—the Lord!

Chapter 1

Practical Living:
How to Make Everyday Choices
(and Stick to Your Choices)

Introduction

As you read this, it is important to understand my view of life. Growing up, my dad and others told me I could not do things because I was disabled. As an adult, I got to make my own choices. Why? I had no guardian. I was able to make mistakes and learn from them.

Since 1992, I met people who have mental health issues who wanted to be as independent as I was. Since 1996, people who have intellectual disabilities have come up to me and said they wanted to do things that people without disabilities do such as get married or have a paper route.

While growing up, I worked hard to get others to let me make my own choices! I know a lot of adults who don't make their own choices. Some people who break the law are not allowed to make their own choices. I think adults should make their own choices. Other adults that don't make their own choices have a guardian or a power of attorney make big choices in their life.

In the following pages:
- First, I share my life.
- Second, I explain how I make my choices.
- Third, I write to the choice maker.
- Fourth, I write to the people assisting and communicating with the choice maker to meet their wants, goals and dreams in healthy ways.

I am a firm believer in:
- Health
- Prevention
- Taking Vitamins
- Eating Healthy
- Exercising
- Taking Prescription Medicine
- Choosing Your Own Doctor

I believe it's everyone's responsibility to be as healthy as they possibly can!

Being healthy includes avoiding:
- Drugs
- Alcohol
- Tobacco

Being healthy includes cutting back on:
- Salt
- Sugar
- Caffeine

I believe powers of attorney and guardians can be good for medical and health reasons. A guardian can deliver messages between the patient and the doctor.

Be Safe

I support the right of adults with disabilities to make their own choices and make their own mistakes. I believe it is important to keep an open mind.

If you are worried that what you are doing is unhealthy or dangerous, you should think about doing something else. If you speak extremely slow or if it is hard to understand what you say, it might be best to have a power of attorney or a guardian. Why? People who can speak clearly and quickly can communicate your needs or wants *quickly*. To a doctor and other professionals, "Time is money!"

I chose to write this book after many people who have mental health issues and intellectual disabilities asked me how I got to do things that their guardian wouldn't let them do. This includes:

- Getting married
- Going to college
- Handling their own money

I thought I could reach more people through my books instead of telling my story to one person at a time. I also thought people could go back and look something up if they didn't remember what I wrote.

This is written from the point of view of the decision maker. If I don't know about something, I ask others who do know. Some information is constantly changing, but the source is the same. So, you can look up the latest information.

Chapter 2

Practical Living: How to Choose

Childhood

I was born with partial seizures. I always felt them coming on. The left side of my body does not work very well. I have a rose-colored birthmark on the right side of my face. I have almost no vision in my right eye. I also have a conceptual learning disability.

I had few friends growing up because my parents were embarrassed by the kids in special education. My parents wanted me to have friends who had no disabilities, but the able-bodied kids teased me. I tried to be friends with all the adults my parents invited over including professionals. I thought I didn't understand. I thought my parents would approve of anyone without disabilities because my parents let them in the house. They didn't approve. My parents were upset with me, but I never understood why they disapproved.

While growing up, I was on many different medicines over the years. I had lots of side effects. Side effects are unwanted things that happen as a result of taking medication. Side effects I had:

- Feeling sleepy all the time
- Hard time focusing
- Hard time understanding schoolwork

A doctor told my mom I would not walk or talk. God proved the doctor wrong. I walk with a limp, but I don't use a walker or a cane. I talk extremely well!

Family Life

One important thing my parents taught me was being faithful to each other and to me when life got hard. My mom had a disability called Multiple Sclerosis (MS). She had a mild case of it. Over the years, her MS had gone in and out of remission. "Remission" means the symptoms of a disability disappear. When the disability comes "out of remission," the symptoms reappear. When I was two years old, my mom had to use a walker because her MS was out of remission. There were times she would have double vision for a week or two, and then her vision was fine again.

When I was in grade school, my mom was a stay-at-home mom. When I entered middle school, she got a job. She worked for about 13 years, then her MS stayed out of remission and she was unable work.

My dad worked at Kaiser Aluminum. He rotated shifts. He worked day shift, swing shift, and the graveyard shift. He also worked a lot of extra hours. My dad had no disabilities. Growing up, my dad and I excessively frustrated each other a lot because we didn't understand each other. That was hard on my mom. For example, I always sang in the school choir. I would tell my dad the date of my upcoming concert 1-3 months in advance of my concert. I thought God and family were more important than a job.

My value system was and still is that God and family are more important than a job. As an adult, I started to understand—you can live in the same house, go to the same church, but still have totally different values.

I have no siblings because my parents were afraid of having another child with disabilities. They have even said to me, "Do you want another disabled child like you in this world?"

This is one of my beliefs: Stand up for what you believe in!

I learned to stand up for myself and voice my opinions. I always knew I was special in God's eyes. Everybody is!

My Grandparents

We visited my grandmother in Idaho often while I was growing up. She was always there for everyone. She was my dad's mom. As her eight kids grew up and moved all across the country, she stayed in contact with everyone. (These were the days before cell phones and the internet.) She was great at having family reunions. She died in a hospital from heart failure when I was in the 7th grade. That was my first experience with death.

I was close to my mom's parents. My grandpa worked on a farm. Grandma was a homemaker. We visited my grandparents frequently. The main thing my grandparents taught me: Family comes first. Whenever they saw their grandchildren, we were the center of their attention and that helped me have strong family values. Later in life, grandpa suffered from Alzheimer's disease and grandma got skin cancer. She died at my aunt's house in 1990, a few weeks after I graduated from high school. My aunt and two cousins took care of them along with an agency called Hospice until grandma died.

My family took care of my grandpa until it got too difficult. My mom and aunt decided to place grandpa into an adult family home. It is *my* belief that the women of the family should take care of their older relatives *if* the family can afford it. We could afford it and I wanted to.

There were a couple of problems with me taking care of him:

- The first problem: No one ever asked my grandpa.
- The second problem: I was told, "You're disabled. You can't take care of him!"
- The third problem: My aunt and mom were assuming my grandpa would be embarrassed if I took care of him.

- The fourth problem: His generation always made sure that the family took care of sick family members even if that meant older relatives had to move into another family member's home.

It would have been respectful *to ask* my grandpa before placing him in the adult family home and later moving him into a nursing home. My grandpa died in early 1993.

After all three of my grandparents died, there were no more family reunions. For a few years after they died, we stayed in touch by calling each other and writing letters. Eventually, the letter writing stopped and later everyone stopped calling each other.

I never let my disabilities get in my way or stop me from doing what I wanted! I wanted to be like everyone else. I wanted to ride a bike, swim, sing in the choir, and play sports. As an adult, I wanted to do all the things other able-bodied adults did such as get a driver's license, move away to college, get a part-time job, and become a wife and a stay-at-home mom. *I wanted to find out for myself what I could or could not do!*

As a kid, I never learned to ride a bike without training wheels, so I don't ride. I think swimming is fun, but swimming alone is dangerous. I remember when I was seven years old in a friend's backyard pool and I had a seizure. A five year old neighbor was keeping my head above water while yelling for her mom to help. The neighbor's mom called my mom. After that, I usually wanted to swim in pools that I could easily get out of. Why? Safety: Because I knew lifeguards were around.

Once you find out something is unhealthy or dangerous, find a healthier and safer way to do it.

"Accommodation" means finding a way that works around your disability or disabilities to allow a person to do things independently. An example would be people who are blind using a white cane or a service animal to walk around.

Church Background

When I was a child, the only reason some of the kids went to church was because they were forced to.

When I entered 10th grade, I met my first boyfriend. He invited me to his church. My parents said I could go. That was October 1987 and I was 16.

**The last five churches I went to were my choice; I chose to leave my parents' religion. They had the right to have their own religion and where they wanted to attend church and so did I! Their religion was different, but it was *not* wrong! I want you to feel good about your choices! My parents allowed me to change churches and I went there for ten years!

School

My mom gave the school my medical information and that bothered me! I felt that only the doctors should have that information. I was afraid the teachers would treat me differently if they knew I had disabilities. I was right! They <u>did</u> treat me differently. My parents and the high school never let me take driver's education! No one ever gave me credit for thinking safely! If I didn't feel safe, I would not drive.

When I was in 3rd grade, a kid said, "F you." So, I asked mom, "What does 'F you' mean?" She slapped me. That was the first time my mom ever hit me. I learned quickly—don't ask my parents questions, hide in the church, and stick with people who have disabilities. Why? Kids without disabilities use profanity. Using profanity got me in trouble. Since I never wanted to be in trouble, I stayed away from kids without disabilities. I was so sheltered that I didn't realize both people with and without disabilities use profanity.

Before I entered 6th grade, my parents moved seven miles off the bus line. As long as I was too young to drive, I thought we should live near a bus route. My parents repeatedly told me that I would never be able to drive. I worried that I would never drive and never have a social life.

My reasons for believing that I could drive was *when* I had a seizure, I stayed alert and I could feel when my seizures were coming on. Since I could feel my seizures coming on, I believed I had enough time to pull over before the seizure was full blown. (It's possible that could have changed over time.)

Throughout middle school, I was mad at God, my parents, and the world. The reason I was so frustrated with my disabilities is because I felt I was being socially isolated.

In 8th grade, a group of female students kept calling me a virgin and I had no idea what "virgin" meant. I kept saying, "No, I'm not!"

They finally asked me, "Who did you sleep with?"

I told them, "Nobody! That's gross!"

They responded, "Then you're a virgin."

I said, "Okay," and I accepted it and wore the term proudly!

Choir, English and math were my best subjects when I was in K-6. My grades in English and choir continued to be great in 7-12. My grades in history were always low. History and social studies were emotionally challenging because of all the guns, war and death.

Biology and science made me feel sick. Dissecting frogs and other things were physically hard, and formulas made no sense. So, I tried to forget everything about those subjects. Teachers gave me a "D" in the difficult classes so I could go to the next grade level. Physical Education was also hard. Why? Catching balls was difficult. I had a hard time running because I sprained my ankle falling on the ice so many times. The only sport I liked in school was volleyball but I still got smacked in the face with the volleyball. I was having fun!

1st through 8th grade, my friends were girls. In 9th through 12th grade, my friends were boys. 10th grade was when I became interested in dating men who went to church.

Remember, if it's hard to do some of the things that I write about, there are agencies out there that can help! If there are other things you need help with, look to see who can teach you. Who you ask depends on what kind of help you need.

The type of help people might need is:

- Advice
- Financial help (help with money) (energy assistance)
- Shopping
- Paperwork
- Homework
- Something else

People or agencies that might be able to help are:

- Family
- Government agencies
- Nonprofit organizations
- Your place of worship or organizations that help people of your faith
- Friends

For example, if I need to get something like milk, or go back to the doctor in the same day, there are a few people I can ask for a ride. If I need help with my homework, I have a different group of people I can ask.

Chapter 3

Taking Medication and Choosing Doctors

Before anyone thinks about living on their own, they need to prove that they know how to take their medication, when to take it, and prove they can be trusted to always take it!

At age 12, my parents trusted me to take my own medication. In the summer of 1986, I went to visit my cousins for seven days. I *accidently* forgot to take my medication. When I realized I had forgotten to take them, I told my aunt. She asked, "Are you having any seizures?" I said, "No."

While my mom was driving us home, I told her I stopped taking my medication and she nearly drove off the road. She was scared saying, "And you are not having withdrawal symptoms or seizures?"

I answered, "No! What are withdrawal symptoms?"

I never should have asked because I trusted God to heal me. However, being the curious person that I am, I asked, "What are withdrawal symptoms?"

I got every symptom she told me about. My parents allowed me to continue taking my medication because I admitted my mistake. No one thought I would stop taking my medication *again*. After all, I'm the one who suffered!

If you are a slow learner, or if you learn by making the same mistakes over and over again, others may want you to have a backup plan.

I graduated in 1990, and I changed my medical doctor. Six to nine months after I graduated, I wanted to be on less seizure medication. My new medical doctor didn't know me well enough and didn't know much about my condition, so he disagreed. Finally, after another six to nine months later, he decided to send me to a doctor who knew more about seizures. If your doctor listens to you and will work with you, ***follow your doctor's advice***!

In 1992, I had an emotional breakdown. I willingly went into the hospital for 14 days and started taking a new medication. Three months later, I asked the doctor if I could stop taking the medication or if I needed it? The ***doctor said*** I could stop!

In 2000, a lot of things were happening.

- The company that manufactured of one my medications stopped making it.
- I got a new neurologist who never respected me.
- I had a personal crisis in my life.
- The disrespectful doctor pushed me over the edge.
- I was getting 2-3 hours of sleep a night for three weeks.

As a result, I accidently did something dangerous and had to get my stomach pumped. Since I was concerned about all the sleep I had lost, I told my counselor four days before I ended up in the emergency room. I was back in the hospital half willingly. Why? I didn't trust my counselor since she didn't believe me when I told her I needed help. She waited too long to get me the help I needed. I was also in a different hospital and they were cruel to me. They took me off of all my seizure medication and when I had a seizure, they told me I was faking it. Those doctors in the hospital should have known what a seizure was even if they didn't know anything about seizure medication. They should have been intelligent enough to talk to my neurologist and never should have taken me off my medication!

In the hospital, I was diagnosed with two more disabilities—bipolar and panic/anxiety disorder. I knew about the panic/anxiety attacks for a long time. I chose not to go to the doctor, and I handled it in a very foolish way. I didn't want to get help.

There was a client at the mental health agency that was the cause of my panic/anxiety attacks, and the agency was legally unable to protect me. What I needed was the agency to make sure our appointments were at different times so we would ***never*** be in the building at the same time. I knew this person went there, and I felt the agency was treating me as if I didn't know anything and/or that they didn't care about my safety! I did get help once my medical insurance allowed me to go to a different agency!

When I got out of the hospital, I was able to take my medication myself. I believe I was allowed to continue taking my medication because I went to my counselor when I was having problems, so my crisis was the agency's fault. If I had said, "I'm fine. I don't need help," when I really did need help, I probably would have had to live in an adult family home until I could be trusted again. Others would have been worried about me and I might have been forced to have a guardian. That is why it is important to know your needs, wants and limitations.

Regarding reducing medication: If you want the doctor to reduce your medication, have a reason! It is the same with changing doctors or avoiding certain doctors—have a reason! Since I have problems with my eyes, it was very stupid of me to go to the eye doctor every 3-5 years. The doctor instructed me to come in every three months. I hate anything in my eyes; however, it is very important for *my vision*. I have finally matured enough to go to the eye doctor every 2-3 years.

The third thing you have to do: *Go to all* of your doctors' appointments. Call ahead of time if you can't make your appointment and schedule a new appointment!

When I moved out of my parents' house, I was in the process of choosing which doctors to keep and which doctors to change. For a while, I saw the same kind of doctor twice for the same thing. He gave my mom and me the information since we were both making different appointments. (I got to the appointments I made by taking the city bus or disability van.)

A year later I switched my doctor because:

- I knew of a doctor in my church
- To start my life separate from my parents

I kept my parents in my life but wanted some distance which is why I got different doctors. When I switched my doctors, I kept it a secret for six months. I wanted my doctors to know me!

TO THE CHOICE MAKER: If you want to be more independent with your medication, talk with your pharmacist and your doctor who prescribes it to you. Questions should include:

- What is this medication for?
- What is it supposed to do for me?
- What are the possible side effects of this medication?
- You must tell the prescribing doctor about _all_ the side effects you have from a medication.

If you have any side effects that you refuse to live with, tell your support team and healthcare professionals what those side effects are so they can find medications that don't have those side effects! For example, there is a new device that can help reduce or stop seizures; however, it would affect my voice. I would rather live with the seizures than mess up my voice because I love to sing. I also hate medication that will make me tired unless the medication is to help me sleep.

Know your boundaries. If you are not taking a medication for the purpose of making you tired, there might be another medication that does the same job but will not cause fatigue.

ALL MEDICATIONS HAVE SIDE EFFECTS!

Regarding taking your own medication:

- Ask if you can take the medication out of the bottle with supervision.
- If you have been taking it out of the bottle correctly with supervision, ask if you can take your medication without supervision. If they say, "No," find out why!

If you want to consider changing doctors, here is one way to do it. There are many ways. This is my way:

1) Look up four doctors.

a) It gives you practice at shopping around for the best of everything (products and services) even when you have the best.
   b) If you do have the best, you will be able to trust your support team even more!
2) Ask friends.
3) When you call a new doctor's office, ask if they will accept your "medical insurance." Make sure you know who your insurance company or companies are *and* that every doctor you have accepts your insurance. If you don't have any medical insurance, ask if they offer a sliding scale fee. If they accept "sliding scale fee," then ask them how much they will charge you!
4) What services does each doctor provide? Do they provide the services that you need?
5) If it is important to you that you and your doctor believe the same way on certain things, then ask them!
6) Has the doctor ever been sued for malpractice?
7) If the doctor has been sued, how many times and for what reason?
8) Finally, ask any questions that are *important to you*! If you need help thinking of some questions, ask your support team to help you think of questions you would want to ask. Your list of questions should reflect your needs, wants and desires.

Personally, I know what kind of doctors I want to have. They are usually in a certain age range. I choose doctors who are a little older. They seem to have more experience and nothing seems to shock or surprise them. I also look at their "personality."

TO SUPPORT TEAM: If the choice maker comes to you and says, "I want to take my own medication," talk it over with them to see if they really understand the responsibility. If they understand, allow them to take it with supervision! If they have been supervised and they ask to take it without supervision, ask them different questions.

If they want to change doctors, give them information about their doctor and other doctors who work in that field! Get four for each kind of doctor that's needed! Find out why they want to change doctors.

TO THE BOTH OF YOU: Talk to each other! Find out why your support team doesn't want you to take your medication at this time and find out why it's important to your choice maker for them to take their own medication. You two might disagree with each other, but if you disagree, find a compromise—something that gives both of you a little bit of what you want.

If the choice maker doesn't want to take prescription medication:

- Get information about alternative medication
- Talk to your doctors if you are interested in trying alternative medication and *before* taking prescription medication!
- Eat healthy
- Take vitamins (Let your pharmacist and all your doctors know what vitamins you want to take and why!)
  If you take vitamins, have your doctor prescribe them to you, so if you ever have to go to the hospital or move into an assistive living facility, you will still get to take your vitamins!
- Exercise

Do all of the above things consistently!

If the choice maker wants to reduce or change medication, tell the doctor the reason that you want to change it, especially if the medication is working. My medication was working but made me so tired that I couldn't do anything. *When* I moved onto the bus line, I noticed how tired I was. As long as I lived in the country with no social life, I never noticed how fatigued I was because I was so bored. If your doctor isn't listening to you, your support team should make the doctor listen and understand you!

The doctor might not be able to give you what you ask for, but if they are smart, they will tell you why!

I became so independent that when I ended up in the hospital in 2000, I didn't have an advocate to tell the hospital staff that I couldn't open childproof medication bottles. Therefore, when I got out of the hospital, I had to find someone who could open my medication bottles for me.

The hospital assumed that since most people enjoy watching TV, I would also. *I hated TV!* Why? Too much sex, violence and profanity! The staff showed no respect for my religious beliefs and no understanding of my physical limitations. When I got out of the hospital, I had to find someone to speak for me in case it happened again!

Part of being independent is knowing **when to ask questions and when to accept help!**

It's smart for everyone to choose two people they can trust to make decisions for them in case they ever become unable to make their own choices.

In order for professionals to know who is allowed to make decisions on your behalf, you must write it on a legal document. The document becomes legal when the document is taken to a notary and signed. The substitute decision maker is only allowed to make decisions when the creator of the document *cannot* make decisions!

If I can't make my own healthcare choices, <u>**I want to choose the person who will make my choices when I can't**</u>!

I HAVE MADE THIS DOCUMENT **and had to use this document a couple of times**!

I feel safe knowing *who* will speak for me if I'm unable to speak for myself!

Chapter 4

Making Choices by Setting Boundaries

We make choices every day. The choices you make create *who you are as a person*. We choose our friends, where we want to live, work, etc. We also make lifestyle choices by the boundaries we set. "Boundaries" mean what you will and will not do. "Boundaries" also mean what you will and will not accept from others. People know who we are by what we will not do. We are also known by who our friends are.

When thinking about what you want your boundaries to be, think about how you were raised. Do you want to do what your family did? I tried to learn from my parents' mistakes and not repeat those mistakes. As time goes by, I would see if I needed to change any of my choices and identify why that choice can be changed. I make new boundaries when I need to.

How does a person choose their boundaries? Find out what you value most. Possible values are your:

- Health
- Faith
- Safety
- Morality
- Etc.

You must set **your** boundaries! Don't give into peer pressure.

This is how I make choices on any subject:

- First, how would I feel if one of my Christian friends knew I was doing this?
- Second, is it healthy?
- Third, is it legal?
- Fourth, can I afford it?

I always listen to how and why other people set the boundaries they have. I won't let anyone force me into their way of thinking. For example, it took me ten years to understand health issues. Now that I understand health issues and why it's important, I am a very strong supporter of being healthy. I respect other people's right to make their own choices even if their choices are unhealthy. However, I have the right to choose friends who make healthy choices.

The only time I will force someone to make healthy choices is if my employer tells me I must! My method is to strongly suggest the reason why it can be a certain way. The more a person means to me, the more it matters to me that they make healthy choices and stay healthy!

Boundaries help us in selecting our friends and hobbies. Boundaries assist us in how we spend our time! When talking to your support team and healthcare professionals, ask them what their boundaries are and how they created their boundaries. *Respect* everyone's right to set their own boundaries. When you have set your boundaries, tell your support team what your reasons are!

Remember your boundaries make up who you are as a person! They tell people what you will accept and what you refuse to accept!

Lifestyle Choices

We all make choices in life. Some choices identify who we are. Our choices tell others if we are:

- Godly or ungodly
- Moral or immoral
- Ethical or unethical
- Professional or unprofessional

Even though it's common practice to respect everybody, we may increase or decrease how much time we spend around people based on the other person's habits and boundaries along with your habits and boundaries. How do you want to be known? The next few chapters will look at some big areas of life.

Choose your lifestyle. Be open to reasonable change. (For example, as cigarettes get more expensive, is it smart to continue smoking? Another example would be changing jobs. If there's a problem at work, do you change departments, look for a different job, or do something else?)

Religion

As a child, I had to go to church with my parents. I had no choice. The church taught me to be a moral person. When I got into middle school, the teenagers at church teased me about my disabilities as much as the teenagers at school did. They teased me about the way I walked and the way I looked. I did not expect to be teased by teenagers at church.

When someone at school invited me to their church in 10th grade, I gladly went! The youth group was big and they did not tease me because of my disabilities. I told my parents I wanted to attend that church. They talked it over and said that would be fine.

Six months after attending that church, I chose to accept Jesus Christ into my heart, instead of only having the knowledge of Jesus Christ in my head. Jesus is the main reason I can smile even though I have multiple disabilities.

How to choose your faith (or not):

- First, realize that this is a personal choice.
- Second, watch people who believe in different religions/faiths. How does faith affect their life? Are they usually happy, sad, angry, stuck up, joyful, and do they look like they have peace?

- Third, choose 10-20 people in each faith and watch them. Why 10-20? To get a consensus and not base your decision on one person.
- Fourth, don't easily change your mind if you are happy with your life!
- Fifth, know yourself well enough to know if a faith will or won't work for you.

Here is an example of one faith that would never work for me. I am a very politically active person, who will stand up for religious values and for the rights of people who have disabilities. There is a religion that avoids politics. That would drive me crazy! I vote and call politicians on the City, County, State, and Federal level. Knowing how politically active I am, I could never be part of that faith! Also, I am perfectly happy with the faith I have, so why look? This is worth saying again! If you are happy with your faith, don't easily change to another faith!

However, it's always smart to watch how your family and friends react when bad things happen (and remember their reactions). How does their faith help them when bad things happen to them?

There are people who share their faith with everyone. You can choose to share your faith, you can keep quiet about your faith until someone asks you, or you can choose to avoid conversations of faith. It's your choice!

Smoking and Vaping

Everyone I knew were nonsmokers until I started middle school. If anyone smoked while I was in elementary school, I didn't know. Therefore, I chose to never smoke.

After I made the choice to never smoke, I found out my dad was a smoker for ten years, and he stopped smoking overnight for my benefit, so I would never start smoking.

Other reasons I chose to be a nonsmoker was, I love to sing and smoking would hurt my voice, and it stinks. I also read in the Bible that the body is the temple of God. Since my body is the temple of God, I don't want to hurt my body!

TO THE CHOICE MAKER: Here are some things to think about when making this choice:

A) First, can you afford to buy cigarettes?
B) Second, smoking can make you get a horrible cough known as "smoker's cough."
C) Third, smoking can cause your teeth and fingernails to turn yellow. When that happens, smokers look older!
D) Fourth, do you want to play music or sports? Smoking makes it very hard to breathe! If you smoke, it will be really hard to succeed in music or sports.
E) Fifth, your health. Smoking makes your lungs black! The longer you smoke, the blacker they get and the harder it will be to breathe. Smoking can cause many lung problems including lung cancer.
F) Sixth, smoking is socially unacceptable.

    It is still legal. All 50 States are trying to make smoking illegal.

    Author's suggestions: If you have a strong opinion about any law the City, County, State, or Federal Government are in the process of creating or modifying, call or e-mail your politicians.

G) Seventh, when I was in 12th grade, the athletes and music students had to sign a contract. The athlete's contract said they couldn't smoke. The music student's contract said nothing in the contract about smoking. However, both athletes and music students got letters in their high school jackets. The coaches complained about there being two different sets of rules, so in the middle of the semester, the choir teacher came into class and said, "If you smoke, you will fail this class!"

It was too late to change classes. As a nonsmoker, I gathered all the smokers together and we went to the vice-principal's office. My main issue was that the teacher was breaking the contract. If students had to obey *the contract*, so did the teachers! If they wanted to change the contract next semester that was fine, but the school had to obey the current contract! We won, and the new contract said music students could not smoke. Why did I help the students? They helped me by signing a petition to get a Bible Club or class. I wanted the Bible Club to be able to advertise just like other clubs did.

H) Eighth, smoking is an addiction. I have a couple of recovering alcoholic friends who are also "recovering smokers." A "recovering smoker" is someone who was addicted to smoking and has stopped smoking but might always be tempted.

Two of my friends told me that to quit smoking is harder than trying to stop drinking alcohol. One has stopped smoking and the other one still smokes. Both my friends explained the process of quitting is like going through mental and physical withdrawal symptoms.

The best way mental withdrawal was explained to me: Smokers always have to have something in their mouth and in their hand. The longer a person smokes the harder it will be for them to quit when they want to.

How can you tell if you are addicted to something? If there's anything you feel like you *have to do* or *can't stop* doing, even if someone else would suffer from it, you are addicted!

There are only two **_possible_** good things I know about smoking:

A) It's a drug that won't alter your mind. Alcohol and *illegal* drugs alter the mind.
B) The second thing I've been told by smokers is that "smoking releases stress." (Those same smokers are

quick to say, "There are healthier ways to deal with stress without smoking!")

If you are thinking about smoking, ask people you trust, "Why did you start smoking?" Ask a number of people before you make your own decision. Chances are, if they still smoke, they really want to quit. (Most smokers I talked to said they started because of peer pressure, wish they had never started, and have quit or want to quit!) Don't start smoking because your friends started smoking!

We can all take steps to live healthier lives by choosing to be nonsmokers, cut back or quit. If you don't smoke, don't start! Being a nonsmoker doesn't promise a long life, it increases your chances of enjoying a healthy life! Through reading this chapter you have learned what questions to ask smokers, ex-smokers, and nonsmokers regarding why they chose to smoke, quit or never start.

Below is the research I did!

I asked smokers and ex-smokers, "Why did you start smoking?" The following is a list of answers I got:

- "It relieves my stress."
- "I do not know."
- "My family smoked when I was a child, so I started smoking."
- "I wanted to fit in with the crowd."
- "Peer pressure."
- "There is no good reason, it's stupid!"

My question to anyone who is thinking about smoking is, <u>why</u> would you want to start? I have only heard of two people who really enjoy smoking. One of these two made weak attempts to stop smoking because his wife nagged him and his child had a breathing problem. I believe smokers must want to quit for themselves to succeed!

If a smoker stops smoking for someone else, they'll probably start smoking again. If someone asks a smoker to stop smoking or never start, please listen to their reason(s) and then make your choice. It's important and polite for smokers to tell others why they don't want to quit. If you want to start smoking, it's smart to tell someone why you are choosing to start.

I 100% accept your choice to smoke, cut back, or not smoke at all. The only thing I ask of smokers is to *please show the same respect for nonsmokers that I am willing to show you*!

RESPECTFUL SMOKING TIPS:

- Don't throw the butts on the ground!
- Throw your cigarettes in ashtrays, *not* on the ground!
- Be polite!
- If you know there is a nonsmoker around, tell them you want to 'light up.' You can ask a nonsmoker to go somewhere else while you smoke because nonsmokers and ex-smokers can go anywhere. Smokers cannot!
- If there are people around you who have a breathing problem, don't smoke around them! Their life depends on being in a smoke-free environment. If you can't wait, go somewhere else to smoke and then come back. If your addiction is so bad that you feel the need to have a cigarette when someone around you is on oxygen, it's time to cut back or quit!
- When "hanging out" with a nonsmoking friend, *ask* them, "Would it bother you if I smoke?" If it would, then don't! If you can't wait any longer, then let them know, go somewhere else, smoke, and when you are done smoking, go back to your friend.
- When you are outside, make sure the smoke is blowing away from people, and not into anyone's face.
- When you are done smoking, **air yourself out** before going back inside!

Vaping cigarettes, pipes and cigars:

For smokers who can't or don't want to quit smoking, there's a new kind of cigarette available. It's a "vapor." There are also electronic pipes and cigars. These products are also called "vapors." Using vapors is called vaping.

If you have to smoke, the main benefit to vaping is there's no risk to the people around you. However, vaping is more dangerous to the person vaping, but the people around you won't suffer from your choice!

Vapors, pipes and cigars:

- Has nicotine. Nicotine is what makes smoking addictive!
- Has no tobacco. Tobacco is the ingredient that causes fires! Using electronic devices will never cause house fires or forest fires.
- Doesn't cause 2nd-hand smoke, so only you smoke!
- It's cheaper in the long run!

I accept everybody's choices regarding smoking no matter what my choices and opinions are because I want other people to accept and to respect my choices and opinions even if they disagree with me!

How do you make the choice to start, cut back, quit, or never start smoking? Go through all the questions listed above and below and see if any of them are important to you. In what ways are they important to you? Are they important in starting, cutting back, or stopping?

Do your own research! You can ask smokers, ex-smokers, and nonsmokers why they made the choice they made. You can also find information from:

- TV
- Internet
- Newspaper/Magazines
- Place of worship
- Family
- Friends
- Healthcare professionals

I was tempted to smoke once. I was 34. I had three reasons to continue to be a nonsmoker. I choose not to reveal my reasons. However, when I was tempted, I talked to a smoker who told me, 'I was smart for never smoking.' That made me feel good! He helped me stay a nonsmoker.

If you have chosen to stop smoking, you need to plan how you will avoid the temptation to start again. You will need to know what made you want to start smoking. Learn to recognize your triggers and avoid or run away from triggers.

Depending on the situation, I deal with my stress, panic/anxiety attacks and anger by praying, reading my Bible, fighting for the rights of people who have disabilities, singing, deep breathing, and going for a walk, etc. The way I lower stress, anxiety, and anger might not help you to lower yours. Find ways that will take your mind off smoking that will help you!

Do you want to say, "No," when someone asks you to go outside and smoke with them? If you want your answer to be "No," find friends who don't smoke. This way you avoid the situation. If you make friends with people who used to smoke, these friends can share with you how they learned to say, "No." They can also encourage you to say, "No."

To the smoker: *Be safe!* Here are some safety tips:

- Never smoke in bed.
- Use a lighter.
- Avoid matches.
- Never let children play with cigarette lighters.
- Always keep lighters and cigarettes **out of reach of children**.
- If you use matches, put them in an ashtray!
- Finish a cigarette or PUT IT OUT!
- *Never leave cigarettes burning when you are done smoking!*
- Make sure cigarettes are out.
- Never throw cigarettes out car windows.
- Never share other people's lit cigarettes.

- Never take cigarette butts out of public ashtrays.

The reason for the last two are to prevent spreading germs. It's not healthy!

TO THE CHOICE MAKER:
- How much does it cost?
- What are the short and long term health risks?
- Are there any benefits to smoking?
- Why did a smoker start smoking?
- Why did people who used to smoke quit smoking?
- Why did the people who never started smoking, never start?

To 2nd-hand smokers:

How do smokers treat you? For example, one of my close smoking friends has chosen to be my telephone friend! Another friend who smokes has never respected me or his wife as nonsmokers. When I stopped going to their house, I found I could breathe better and smell things. If you are looking for a romantic relationship, would it bother you to kiss an ashtray? A smoker's mouth is like an ashtray. If it would bother you, don't get into a romantic relationship with a person who smokes.

TO SUPPORT TEAM: With all the information there is telling people that smoking is bad and to say, "No," to smoking, they don't need to be told by you also. Let them make their own choice. If they choose to smoke, you can let them know that you disagree with their choice, but that you respect their right to make that choice. This will give them a chance to be more open minded to change their mind if they don't like the consequences.

Alcohol

What is alcohol? Alcohol is a *legal* drug. Alcohol is a major ingredient found in beer, wine, liquor, some prescription medication, and some over-the-counter medication. Alcohol Pamphlet: Performance Resource Press, Inc., Troy, Michigan 1-800-453-7733. (Referred to as "Alcohol Pamphlet" from now on.)

What does alcohol do to a person? Lowered self-esteem and "lowered self-control often leads to loud or aggressive behavior." (Alcohol Pamphlet)

Alcohol can change what reality looks like. 'Alcohol can temporarily make a person's sight, hearing, feeling, smelling, and taste buds bad.' Alcohol *can* affect a person's memory, muscle coordination, and judgment. "The bigger the dose, the greater the damage." 'In large doses...effect on the brain can also cause coma, unconsciousness, respiratory failure, and death.' (Alcohol Pamphlet)

A question I had: "If alcohol is so dangerous, why has our elected officials allowed alcohol to continue to be legal?" I did get an answer, but the answer is too hard to explain.

I interviewed seven people about alcohol. The questions are about their personal experiences and their opinions about alcohol.

I interviewed a couple of "recovering alcoholics." My first interview was with a man in his early 40's. This man started drinking alcohol by choice after he had surgery because he was in pain. He wanted off his pain medication. Why? His girlfriend said she would marry him if he stopped taking his prescribed medication. Against the doctor's advice, he stopped taking the medication and started drinking alcohol to stop his pain. He thought he would know when to stop drinking.

I thought, 'There must be a mix of good and bad things to drinking alcohol because so many people try to quit drinking while others are starting at the same time.' It's been this way throughout history.

Continued first interview: "As an outsider looking in, what do people think is so fun about drinking?"

He said, "Nice feelings such as loosening up, like taking pain medicine and it is nice on social occasions."

"What are the downsides of drinking alcohol?"

"Getting a hangover, feeling sick the following day. You lose your health because your body does not get the nutrients it needs. You can also lose your family and your job."

"How long has it been since you had your last drink?"

"Eleven years with no relapses at the time of this interview."

"What took you so long before you chose to quit drinking?"

"I got sick three times. The third time I decided to quit because my stomach hurt so much. When I chose to stop drinking, I was given a prescription medicine to take away the good feelings of drinking, and I went into an outpatient treatment program Monday–Friday from 8:00am–5:00pm. The doctor made sure I was ready to stop drinking before he prescribed me that medicine to help me quit. The continuing support or support systems are helping me to stay sober, counseling and going to Alcoholics Anonymous (AA)."

Another couple of questions I asked was, "Is there any such thing as 'responsible drinking'?"

"Absolutely! You **cannot** be an alcoholic **and** a responsible drinker at the same time!"

"Do you have any other comments?"

"If you take prescription medicines, *don't* drink!" End of interview.

Alcohol affects people differently. Physical, mental, and environmental factors are some of the ways that will determine how people react to alcohol. Another factor is, do they have food in their stomach at the time of consumption, how much they weigh, their tolerance level, their personality, and their mood. (Alcohol Pamphlet)

What is social drinking? The term "social drinker/social drinking" can be very confusing. Why? Words like "social," "socializing," and the words like "drinker" or "drinking."

To find out what a social drinker really is, let us look to the doctor's opinion. Social drinkers don't drink every day! When they do drink, they space their drinks out by a minimum of one hour.

If you want to drink, for medical reasons, talk to your pharmacist. The pharmacist is an expert on how prescription medication and over-the-counter medication interact with alcohol. Ask a pharmacist, even *before* you drink **red** wine!

Here's the interview of the second person. It is important to know that this man worked 40 or more hours a week. He worked different hours every week.

"Personally, is there anything you consider dangerous about social drinking?"

He said, "Not regarding 'responsible drinking.'"

He also said, "Addiction. There is **always a chance** of addiction."

"How would a person stay responsible about drinking?"

"Read the danger signs such as being in trouble with the law, money problems, or having bad thoughts about yourself while you're still drinking!"

His advice is, don't drink if you're in trouble with the law, have money problems, or feel bad about yourself.

**Here are three examples that he gave me of "being responsible."

- A) "If you need to drive somewhere, don't drink!" (In my opinion, if you already had a drink and you need to go somewhere, take the bus, disability van, or a taxi cab. Other possibilities are calling a friend to drive you or walk.)
- B) "If you are angry, don't drink. Wait until your anger is gone. Alcohol will make your anger worse."
- C) "If you feel bad about yourself, don't drink. Alcohol is a drug that makes people feel sad."

He is now 70 years old. He has not had a drink in 15-20 years because alcohol caused him to have headaches when he drank. He started drinking for social reasons at age 16. He just wanted to experiment and be cool by fitting in with his friends.

My next few questions are about the nice feelings of how alcohol makes a person feel. "Personally, is there anything you consider enjoyable about social drinking?"

He said, "Yes."

"What is it?"

"Releasing inhibitions and lightening of the spirit."

"Are there any sensations?"

"Flying with the eagles and lightening of the spirit."

In talking with this man, I found out his job was very stressful. He rarely got Saturday and Sunday off. He would come home from work, usually on *his* Friday, and sit down with one or two cans of beer before bedtime. He would sit alone and watch TV to relax. Once he relaxed, he'd go to bed!

These people should not drink:

- Pregnant women!
  If a pregnant woman drinks, the unborn baby is also getting the alcohol into its bloodstream.
- People under age 21!
  In most states, it is unlawful to drink under age 21.
- People who are chemically dependent!

Look at all three of the recovering alcoholic interviews to find out why it is bad for people who are recovering to drink. There are also people who may choose not to drink for health, religious, and personal reasons. (Alcohol Pamphlet)

People have different religious and personal beliefs. People also have different health problems and have to take different medication so they might choose not to drink for health reasons.

It is dangerous to drink and drive. Drink **or** drive. **Never** drink and drive at the same time!!

Is there any danger to social drinking? Yes! "Even one or two drinks slow down judgment and reaction time, so does a hangover." (Alcohol Pamphlet) One of my friends told me that one out of four social drinkers were alcoholics.

The third interview is with a female. She is 30-40 years old. She has never taken a drink of alcohol except for communion at church.

Starting with her childhood thoughts about alcohol, she assumed all alcohol was bad and all people who drank alcohol were bad. She thought alcohol caused all people who drank to be abusive and mean. She changed her mind because she learned the difference between a light and a heavy drinker.

As a teenager, she chose not to drink because she wanted to drive. She thought her parents would let her take driver's education if she made smart choices. She was wrong! They didn't!

Second, she thought drinking when you are underage was wrong. Her religious belief was to obey the law and one of the laws says you must be 21 or older to drink legally. She asked a student pastor before she turned 21, "I am going to be 21 years old and feel that drinking is wrong, but I don't know why. What do you think?"

He said, "If it is not good for a child, then why is it good for an adult?"

She liked the way he left her with something to think about by kindly giving her opinions and didn't react negatively to her questions.

She was physically distant from her family members who were alcoholics and recovering alcoholics. She saw the results of two popular teenage boys three years after she made the choice to never drink. The boy she cared about dropped out of school after the 11th grade. The other boy turned to *illegal* drugs. She did not know anyone who ever killed someone because they drove drunk.

At age 43, I, the author, reconsidered my views regarding different kinds of alcohol.

- I have different reasons why I drink or avoid each of the following: liquor, beer, white wine, and red wine.
- I can get the same flavor or taste from liquor as I can from a nonalcoholic drink when I choose to drink. A nonalcoholic drink is called a virgin drink.
- I have never drank beer! Every time I thought about drinking beer, I wanted to escape problems.

I heard that wine has medical benefits, so I did more research. I found out there's white and red wine. There's no research that white wine has medical benefits therefore I refuse to drink white wine!

Regarding red wine: This is the wine that people are referring to when they say alcohol is good for medical reasons. I did my personal research. Even if my doctor or pharmacist say drinking red wine is bad for me, I might drink red wine anyway; but I would only drink what any doctor says is the correct amount! However, if drinking red wine is the only thing stopping me from getting my driver's license, I WON'T DRINK!

*Do your own research on alcohol!
*Don't trust my research alone!
I'm not an expert!

Why do people drink? "People may choose to drink for cultural, religious, medical, social or personal reasons... Most alcohol use is for social purposes, to relax at get-togethers or to celebrate an occasion. Some people use alcohol to forget worries for the moment or to escape reality." (Alcohol Pamphlet)

Drinking to forget or to escape reality is one of the warning signs that you are headed for problems with alcohol and may lose control.

When I thought about being a light social drinker, I made the choice never to drink in a bar! Why? I don't enjoy visiting with people who have been drinking! No matter what my choice is I need to take responsibility for all my choices! I did my own research and made an educated choice!

My fourth interview was with a 30-40 years old female social drinker. At age 14, she started to experiment with alcohol. When she became of legal age, the reason she chose to be a social drinker was for family and social gatherings. She also liked the buzz; the stepping out of herself. Later in life, she decided she liked to be alone when she drank, so she only drank at home. She never drank as a way to escape reality.

"Is there anything you consider enjoyable about social drinking?"

"Yes."

"What is it?"

"Looser feelings...stepping out."

"Is there anything you consider dangerous about social drinking?"

"Yes."

"What is it?"

"Choosing to drink and drive at the same time...and becoming addicted to alcohol."

"Do you believe it's possible to be a responsible drinker?"

"Yes."

"Can people become dependent on alcohol?"

"Yes."

Alcohol causes mental and physical dependence and can mess up your emotions badly. (Alcohol Pamphlet)

"When a drinker uses alcohol as an escape from problems and stress – and have come to depend on alcohol for relief, they have developed psychological or mental dependence on it. The more they drink, the more alcohol they think they need. The body requires more alcohol to function, and physical dependence has developed. Once dependent, drinkers experience withdrawal symptoms when they stop drinking." (Alcohol Pamphlet)

My fifth interview was with a nondrinker who was 50-60 years old! He told me, "At age 15, a friend stole some alcohol. My friends and I drank it. They also broke the law in other ways that night. I got drunk twice with my buddies, and I got sick both times. My parents wanted me to get new friends. I didn't listen. I chose to join their group. After getting drunk twice, I decided it was more fun babysitting the drunks by being the designated driver."

"Why?"

"I thought it was more fun watching them act stupid and keeping all of them safe."

He stopped being the designated driver when they asked him to do *illegal* drugs. Two of his friends died from alcoholism.

When he lived in California, he got drunk at a house and got sick again. At the request of his friend, he had to physically force him to stop drinking! If that man didn't stop drinking, he was *going to die*! His friend knew he would die, but he had zero discipline to stop on his own! The man I interviewed made a choice at age 20, "If I never take another drink, I cannot become an alcoholic."

Later in life, he met a lady who could not move from the neck down because she was hit by a drunk driver when she was eight years old. She died at age 37.

An alcoholic is a person who has a drinking problem. Alcoholism is a disease. Alcoholics don't know when they have had enough or too much to drink. However, getting drunk over and over again is too much! Alcohol can kill. "Most alcohol deaths are due to very bad injuries, illnesses and the organs in their body being damaged over the years. Even light drinkers can die from respiratory failure after drinking a large amount of alcohol. Severe alcohol withdrawal can also cause death. When alcohol is combined with prescription and/or over-the-counter drugs, there's a higher chance of it killing them." (Alcohol Pamphlet)

The sixth person I interviewed was a female recovering alcoholic. She was between 50-59 years old. She started drinking at age 19 because it was socially acceptable. Her family drank and it was also in her family environment, therefore, it is in her bloodstream. Since her family drank, that is how she was taught to handle stress and that is called "environment."

"Did you choose to stop drinking or were you forced to stop by the court system, by the Developmental Disabilities Administration system, or by the Mental Health system?"

"I chose to quit."

"Why?"

"I was aware of what alcoholism was, so I set up some boundaries for myself, so if I crossed those boundaries I would quit or get help to quit." When she chose to stop drinking, she realized that she could not stop and had a chemical imbalance.

"How did you stop drinking?"

"First, I went to a couple of AA meetings, then to a treatment center for three months. When I got out of there, I went to AA meetings for one year and now I go only when I need to."

"Why did it take you so long before you chose to quit?"

"I reached my personal limit."

"How long did you drink?"

"At the time of this interview, I am not drinking." (Before this book was put in print she did start drinking again.)

If someone becomes a recovering alcoholic, there's hope. However, life will be much more difficult. It is possible for recovering alcoholics to go to school and/or keep a job. These things are easier to get and keep when a person realizes they have a drinking problem. It helps to change their ways when they are not being forced against their will to change.

My seventh interview was with a male recovering alcoholic. He was 50-59. He tried alcohol one time at age 5. He started drinking regularly at age 13. He and his friends broke the law by stealing alcohol and getting drunk.

"How long did you drink?"

"Twenty-three years."

"Why did you stop drinking?"

"At age 35, my oldest daughter was born. I did not want her seeing or living in the environment of violence and anger caused by alcohol."

"Do your children have less of a chance of becoming an alcoholic because they were raised in an alcohol-free environment?"

"Yes, but my children still have a predisposition to alcohol."

"Did you choose to stop or were you forced to stop drinking?"

"I chose to."

"Why did you choose to quit?"

"I quit for my kids' sake."

"What took you so long before quitting?"

"I did not want to. I knew I had a problem. I just didn't care."

"How long have you been sober?"

"Over 17 years."

"Any relapses?"

He said, "Not since I have been in AA."

"Does having a history of alcoholism make college and/or employment easy, difficult or make no difference?"

"The first five years of being sober was hell because I was setting new boundaries and making new friends. After five years of being sober, it was easier."

"Why after five years?"

"After five years, it was easier because I made new friends who helped me stick to the new boundaries I set for myself, since I decided alcohol is 100% off limits to me!"

"As an outsider looking in and having no experience, why do people think drinking is so fun?"

He said, "Fun, socialization, and partying…these are the main reasons. It also helps break up the boredom."

"What would you want me to say are the bad things?"

"Vomiting, hangover, having sex with someone you don't even know, not caring about yourself…stop taking care of yourself, your family, job, and personal business."

Alcohol becomes the most important thing in an alcoholic's life!

"Is there any such thing as a 'responsible drinker'?"

"Yes, there is. Absolutely!"

"Who can?"

"The person who has only one or two drinks or the person

who stops drinking when they start feeling the effects of alcohol is a 'responsible drinker' and/or has no negative effects from drinking."

Alcoholics cannot be responsible drinkers!

"Did you need any supports personally or professionally when you quit?"

"Yes."

"What were they?"

"AA meetings, conferences, Dr. Milam, and reading the book *Under the Influence*."

"Do you have any other comments?"

"The main reason teenagers choose to drink alcohol is peer pressure and wanting to fit in with the crowd."

Think before you make choices because you will live with the results—good or bad!

If you have a problem with alcohol, you can get help from a counselor or a treatment center. "In addition, research show the support of other recovering persons such as those in Alcoholics Anonymous can help people get sober and keep their sobriety." (Alcohol Pamphlet)

"If you suspect you have a drinking problem you can get information and guidance from your medical doctor, your nearest drug treatment center, a local school system, or mental health center. You can find these places online or in the phonebook by looking up 'Alcoholism,' 'Drug & Addiction Services,' 'Family Counselors,' and/or 'Mental Health Services.'" (Alcohol Pamphlet)

TO THE CHOICE MAKER: Now that you have some information from an alcohol pamphlet and have read seven interviews of how others made their choice and what the results were, you can make an educated choice.

If you still need more information, ask your support team, doctor, pharmacist, caregivers, people at your place of worship (if applicable), and close friends who care about you!

Here's a list of questions:

- Do you take prescription medication? If yes, talk to your pharmacist, with your support team quietly at your side.
- If you are in high school and want to drink, will coaches or teachers let you participate in activities?
- Are you curious about alcohol?
- Are you afraid of the way alcohol would make you feel?
- Do you think there are health benefits to drinking alcohol?
- Have you done the research on health benefits and health risks to drinking alcohol?
- Do you want to spend your money on alcohol?
- Is becoming addicted to alcohol worth the risk of drinking?
- What are your religious beliefs regarding alcohol?
- Have you had family members or friends killed by drunk drivers?
- What do you know about drinking safely such as keeping yourself and the community safe while drinking?
- Which is more important, getting a driver's license or drinking?
- Do you know anyone who abuses alcohol?
- How do you think other drinkers behave? How do they look? For example, do they look like they are having fun, angry, happy, sad, hateful, having a good time, etc.?
- What is your value system?
- How would you protect yourself from getting addicted?
- How are you going to protect yourself from being a drunk driver?
- How are you going to stay safe while you are drinking and not fall into the wrong crowd?
- Finally, if you still want to drink, why? State your reasons.

TO SUPPORT TEAM: I realize if you are a power of attorney or a guardian, you have wisdom and that's why a judge gave you the responsibility until he/she can make educated choices. However, he/she will never get the chance to learn new information and use it if they never get to ask experts questions. They need to become educated and make their own decisions. Without asking questions, they won't learn!

Sometimes, it's easier to respect someone's "forced choices" when the support team tells the individual how the choices are being made! For example, how did the support team make their decisions about drinking?

I would also suggest answering the same set of questions *with them* before they have answered them. Tell them if they have a predisposition to alcohol. If so, how many relatives are addicted?

TO THE BOTH OF YOU: Alcohol is a serious topic! When talking to each other, **listen to each other**! It is very important for each of you to understand why you each have the opinions that you have!

Illegal Drugs

I never considered taking *illegal* drugs. Why? It's against the law. I'm a person who always followed the rules as I was growing up. As long as *illegal* drugs are against the law, I won't take them. Second, I take prescription medication. I don't want to take any unnecessary drugs.

Over-the-counter medications are legal as long as you follow the instructions. However, always talk to *your pharmacist* about every over-the-counter medication before taking it. They know what over-the-counter medications work best with the medications you take.

How can you tell if a drug is legal? Legal drugs are medications that doctors prescribe and that you pick up at the pharmacy or that you can buy at a store.

The only reason I'm writing about *illegal* drugs is because there are bad people in the world that might ask you to try them.

You need to know how you want to answer *before* you are asked!

I was shocked to find out that most *illegal* drugs have the *same dangers*! I thought the dangers would be different for each one! I got my information from pamphlets, TV, and talking to recovering drug addicts. A possible benefit or reward of avoiding *illegal* drugs is getting financial aid if you choose to go to college! People who want to be in the military must have avoided *illegal* drugs! *Illegal* drugs affect every user differently! Users will probably not get every side effect, but they cannot choose which side effects they will get and which ones they won't!

Illegal drugs cause the body and the brain to be damaged. A person who uses could:

- get heart failure or an increased heart rate.
- have breathing problems, breathe too fast, or their lungs could fail and they will die.
- risk kidney problems or failure.
- have increased or low blood pressure.
- get hepatitis or AIDS from dirty or shared needles. Dirty needles increase the danger of getting AIDS or hepatitis. There is **no** cure for AIDS! If you get AIDS, you will eventually die!
- get sick more frequently from colds, flus, viruses, or diseases.
- have drug induced seizures (not epilepsy) that can kill quickly. Epileptic seizures are different than a seizure(s) from a "drug overdose." (If you have any questions, ask *your* doctor.)
- possibly lose the desire to eat.
- vomit over and over.
- feel like they are going to faint.
- have insomnia.
- be put to sleep. (Michael Jackson used *illegal* drugs to get some sleep. He died because of it!)

- lose their balance and/or stumble.
- have blurred vision.
- have headaches or muscle aches.
- have pain in their face from unknowingly grinding their teeth.
- have trouble concentrating.
- have long-term or short-term memory problems or no memory at all.
- forget what they did while under the influence. **If** you break the law, you still have to go to jail/prison and/or pay fines.

*I have met three people with memory problems. Most *illegal* drug users build up a tolerance causing a (real or imagined) need to take more and more *illegal* drug(s) to get the same high. This is called a physical addiction! A person who uses:

- can lose their awareness of touch and pain.
- may have urine/bowel issues.
- might get skin rash.
- could damage their nose permanently if *illegal* drugs are snorted. *There is nothing doctors can do to fix the damage!*
- can get a fever.
- may lose concern for their health by not eating or sleeping.
- can have problems with slurred speech or the words might be clear, but their sentences might not make sense to the listener.
- might have a coma which can be deadly.
- could be killed from taking an *illegal* drug one time!

Here are the dangers to your emotions, self-control, and mind. (The following side effects can be symptoms of a mental illness or side effects from taking *illegal* drugs.) If a person already has a mental illness and they use *illegal* drugs, their symptoms can be much worse. Some people get a mental illness because of taking *illegal* drugs. Mental illness is another disability. There are people who have mental illnesses who have never taken *illegal* drugs! A person who uses:

- can lose some of their emotional control.
- can get depression.
- can just lose control.
- can have anxiety attacks, panic attacks, or paranoia.
- can become very suspicious.
- can become confused.
- can have flashbacks.
- can be more irritable.
- might lose interest in food, family, friends, and other activities.
- might have a sense of distance or estrangement.
- might have an over stimulated nervous system.
- can have delusions and/or hallucinations.
- can get a distorted or false view of reality!
- can have schizophrenic-psychosis behavior.
- can get schizophrenia that lasts a lifetime. There are people who have schizophrenia who have never taken *illegal* drugs!
- can get chronic/constant psychosis.
- can get toxic psychosis.
- can have violent behavior, be involved in bizarre accidents or violent crimes.
- can have impaired judgment!
- might have a slow mental processing system.
- might forget who they were before taking drugs.
- may have "catatonic symptoms." Catatonic means the person becomes unable to talk, lethargic, disoriented (confused about their surroundings), and makes meaningless movements or any combination of the four.
- may forget what it was like to live life without taking *illegal* drugs.

*IF a user:

- feels the need to take *illegal* drugs every day, they are addicted physically and/or mentally.
- continues to use *illegal* drugs while taking prescription medication, the user will probably have more severe side effects!
- drinks alcohol **and** takes *illegal* drugs, their side effects will probably be much worse!

Doctors went to school to learn how to make people well! Pharmacists went to school to learn how all drugs work together! If you don't tell your doctor and pharmacist everything they ask you, they can't help you. *So, if you have two or more doctors prescribing you medications, tell all your doctors what medications you are taking and go to one pharmacy!!*

- IF a woman is pregnant and uses *illegal* drugs, she might have a stillborn baby.
- A woman who is pregnant and using *illegal* drugs can also deliver a child with severe disabilities.
- Users don't have money! The reasons are:
  1) Users have a difficult time keeping a job because they have problems showing up on time for work or they forget to show up for work. Why? Their addiction takes control of their life.
  2) *Illegal* drugs are very, very expensive. They are so expensive that users eventually stop paying their rent/mortgage, electricity bill, phone bill, and stop buying food because they don't have enough money to pay the bills and buy *illegal* drugs!

One of my Christian friends stayed off drugs for years and he died about a year ago when he was offered drugs again *and took the offer*!
Please don't!!
Finally, doing *illegal* drugs puts users at risk of losing:

- Family
- Friends
- Job
- Health
- Faith

Why? *Illegal* drugs become the most important thing in a user's life!

Therefore, for the protection of the individual's physical, emotional, social, mental, and possibly spiritual health, I won't give my blessing to *choose illegal* drugs!

My #1 concern would be: Losing my freedom by going to prison!

Chapter 5

Learning How to Budget Your Money

I approach the subject of money with caution. It is too easy to go into debt. Therefore, think carefully where and when you spend your money. A budget is a plan that helps you wisely spend your money.

I have been managing my own money for 21 years. When I was single, I never signed a contract unless my parents said it was okay! Now that I'm married, I won't sign a contract unless my husband says it's okay. *That's my choice*!

If the people you trust tell you that signing something is a bad idea, *don't sign it*! However, find out why later, but not in front of a salesperson! Here's a list of things my parents, my church, or a disability agency taught me about budgeting money.

My parents have always been great at budgeting money and they were great at teaching me how to budget my money. They taught me by giving me an allowance and by paying me for the chores I did around the house. They also taught me how to save and to spend it wisely!

As I grew older, my parents said they would give $10 to a store for every $1 that I gave to the store toward a new bedroom set. I still have most of my bedroom set today.

My parents did this for three reasons:

A) To teach me budgeting skills.
B) They didn't know what my future husband's budgeting skills would be.
C) They also knew that most people live paycheck-to-paycheck. My parents were not rich, but they knew how to pay their bills off quickly so they could buy more things and avoid paying excessive interest.

A disability agency that taught independent living skills also taught me how to budget money while getting a government check. They realized my budgeting needs were different. My needs included: Needing to know what questions to ask a salesperson, how to know if a price is reasonable, and when to and not to buy something that's "on sale."

They taught me to ask myself the following four questions to find out if the product or service that's "on sale" is something I should buy at the time of the sale:

1) Are all my bills paid?
2) Can I afford it?
3) How often will I use the product or service?
4) Can I wait for the next sale?

Ask yourself the four questions above to decide if what's on sale is a good deal *for you*! If you are not going to use a product very often and you need it, can you borrow it instead of buying it or will you use it enough times to make it worth the price?

Here is something I bought at a garage sale—a blue vase.

1) Yes, all my bills were paid.
2) Yes, I needed it because I had caught a bride's bouquet.
3) Yes, I wanted it, and yes, it would be used.

Therefore, it was a good sale for me! Because I started learning how to budget money at a very young age, I never needed a protected payee!

The basics of budgeting your money is to pay your bills first, then you can do what you want with the rest of your money.

"Required bills" means bills that you **must pay**! There are five monthly bills!

1) Rent/mortgage! You must have a place to live.
2) Electricity
3) Telephone
4) Food: You must buy enough food for yourself, so you don't run out before your next check comes. Don't include eating at restaurants.

5) Transportation: The cheapest transportation is walking and riding a bike. If you don't want to walk or ride a bike all over town, you need money to ride the city bus, the disability van, or drive. The next chapter talks about transportation.

At age 16, I started going to a different church that teaches giving *some* money to God. I didn't start giving money to God until I was 23 years old. If you decide to give money to God, you should add that contribution to your budget.

Remember these were *my* choices and *my* opinions and you need to be responsible for *your* own choices and opinions!

Handling Your Money

There are different ways to handle money. The most common way is with a **checking account**. Banks and credit unions are "financial institutions." They will give you a little booklet called a check registry to write down every time you deposit or withdraw money from your account.

Deposit means putting money into an account. **Withdrawal** means taking money out of your account such as when you pay bills. Make sure you fill out everything on a check including signing it.

If you can't remember to write down ***every transaction*** you deposit or withdraw money from your account, you'll never know how much money you have in your account! Why? Money doesn't come out of a checking account until someone cashes the check! It would be smart to get a different kind of account! I know I forget to write everything down, so I will never get a checking account.

A **debit card** is another way to pay your bills and buy things. A debit card won't let you spend more money than you have in your account. If you are interested in a debit card, call your financial institution and ask them. Most people have chosen to use a debit card because the money comes out of your account immediately, and you don't have to wait for the business to cash the check. The business has their money and you know how much you have left if you write it down quickly!

Saving Money

A **savings account** is an account with a financial institution. You deposit money into the account and usually don't withdraw it until there's enough money to buy an expensive item. Money can also be taken out when there's an emergency.

I strongly believe in saving money. By saving money, when my friend found a sale, he bought four Bibles for the four criminals that hurt his daughter. (He chose to buy them Bibles instead hating them because hating them would not undo the damage they caused.)

Money orders look like checks that you buy, but the difference is that this is money that's in an account! I'd rather pay for things by money order or cash instead of having a protective payee or taking the chance of bouncing a check by writing a check for more money than I have in my checking account. **Bouncing a check is also called an overdraft.** The cost of one overdraft is more expensive than the cost of buying money orders.

My parents had an account at a credit union for many years, so I opened up my savings account there. Even though my parents chose to leave the credit union, it is still a good place to do business. *People choose to change where they do business for a variety of reasons including:*

- Better prices
- The customer or business moves
- Another financial institution offers something you need that the other business doesn't offer

Credit Cards

Using a credit card is a form of borrowing money. It's borrowing from a financial institution. Anything that you charge on a credit card **must be paid back!** IF a person does not pay their credit card bill, the financial institution will take the credit card away, and the money will still have to be paid back; no matter what the reason is for using it!

My parents only told me that credit cards were bad, but they never told me why. I wanted to find out if there were good reasons for owning a credit card *before* I made my choice. I chose to get one! When I got **one** credit card, I chose **carefully** *when to use it*! I only used it once in a while!

After researching credit cards, *my personal opinion* is that credit cards are good for emergencies and going on vacation. Sometimes, I buy something using the credit card when I don't have any cash in my purse. I use my credit card and next time I go to the credit union I pay the credit card bill. Sometimes, I pay the bill before it shows up in the mailbox.

If you learn how to manage and budget your savings and/or checking account, it might be safe to get one credit card! If you need or want a credit card, learn your financial institution's language and what each word means. Ask your support team.

When I was thinking of making an expensive purchase using my credit card, I **<u>chose</u>** to take a friend with me to financially protect me. One of my purchases was a recliner for a 20-year old relative! After I paid off the recliner, I wanted to buy a living room set to match the recliner! I paid the bill off quickly!

Traveler's checks can be tracked. People use traveler's checks when they travel.

Gambling

In my opinion, gambling is stupid, but not against my religious beliefs. (I don't know how to explain it. Ask your support team.) Television makes it look wonderful. It's not! When I was 12 or 13 years old, I was interested in gambling. My mom said gambling was a waste of money. She said, "Gambling is like throwing your money away."

Finally, one day when I was about 15 years old, she found a winning ticket worth $2 that someone had thrown on the ground. She picked it up and gave me the choice to keep the cash or to buy two more tickets. If we won any money, it would be mine. I chose to buy two more tickets. We lost the $2. My mom said, "If we had just cashed in the ticket, you would have been $2 richer."

I decided my mom might be right, but I had to ask some people in my church before I made my final decision. The people at church and my mom told me that there's a better chance of losing money. A few people win, but most people lose. If you lose, you also lose the money that you spent to buy the tickets. So, in my early 20's I decided gambling was a waste of money. I've made a choice to never gamble! (I've only gambled one time as an adult!) Gambling to me is foolish, but is not against my religious beliefs or health beliefs, etc.

Lending Money to Friends

I was taught that if I give money to friends or strangers, they would want to be my friend only for my money and strangers might see me as an easy target. I have lent money to friends when I lacked the judgment of what was a need and what was a want! However, my bills were *always paid when* I loaned the money! In one case, it was hard to get my money back because my friend's payee was unwilling to pay me back. I finally did get paid back! How? I talked to the payee's co-worker. I wanted the payee to know that it was *his* client's idea to pay me back. I got paid back, but the payee gave my friend a difficult time for it.

There are also some family members who try to force their values onto their recipients who needs a protective payee. It is illegal for someone to force you to accept their values! However, it's legal and healthy to share your values with others and for others to share their values with you!

*The above situation taught me to never lend money to anyone who has a protective payee. It's okay to *give* money to someone who has a payee, but never lend it.

Borrowing Money

Borrowing is the opposite of lending. Borrowing is very bad. Why? Any time a person borrows money they are in debt! If you borrow money from a friend and they need the money when you are unable to pay them back, that's unfair to them!

If you need money, it is best to borrow it from a financial institution. They charge money for lending customers money. The charge for borrowing their money is called interest. (Ask your support team what interest is. I don't know how to explain it.)

The main reason people get a loan is to buy very expensive things such as a house or to go to college. Loan is a different word for borrowing money. Financial institutions usually give loans based on how much money a person makes (and other reasons) so the lender can decide whether the borrower is financially able to pay them back.

Giving Money to People

I gave money to a friend once in the form of paying her phone bill! I only did this once! I paid her phone bill for four reasons.

- A) Since we talked to each other daily for hours at a time, we wouldn't have been able to talk to each other for a few months!
- B) My friend was very, very responsible with money, but she got into trouble one month. I gave it as a gift and not as a loan.
- C) She did not ask me! She's paid her bills every month since I paid her phone bill. That was over five years ago.
- D) All <u>my</u> bills were paid at the time. I *chose* to pay her bill!

Paying my bills every month is why I don't have a protective payee! A payee can be helpful for some people. Getting your bills paid needs to be your primary rule!

There are bills that are optional. Optional bills in this book means things you have or want, but you can live without even if you are addicted to it.

Below is a true story which explains why it's very important to know who your *real* friends are!

My second fiancé had invited his friend into my apartment, and I wanted him to leave and never come back! I knew him from middle school and high school, and he gave me the creeps. I distrusted him, and I never found out why. My fiancé insisted he stay, so I let the guy in.

Here's what happened: I set money aside to give to church. While I was in the bathroom, he stole my money. I told the thief he stole money I was giving to the church! I told him, that was God's money and it was between God and him! The point: Be smart when choosing friends!

He took advantage of the situation. I told my fiancé to choose between that thief and me, and he chose the thief. Why? He hates confrontation! By choosing to never let that man in my apartment again, I was setting a boundary that protected my property! The above example is what I mean by explaining to your support team *why* you do or don't want someone to be your friend.

Some people want to own a home instead of renting. Owning a home is very expensive because of the cost of maintenance, insurance, etc. Everybody has to save their money for the things they want in life! Are you paying all your required bills before your optional bills? Most people say they can't live without a television, therefore they have cable or dish no matter how expensive it is.

If you believe in giving money, you will want to write it down as a bill. It may go to a religious place or a nonprofit organization like The Arc. The rest of your money is your money! Money you may save or spend! If you don't have enough money, get a job.

I have the attitude that you ***never stop learning*** no matter who you are! It doesn't matter if a person has the worst disability you've ever seen or if a person is a genius. Everyone learns new things every single day! No one is perfect, so when someone makes a mistake, it's an opportunity for them to learn from their mistake(s) through **natural consequences**! Don't protect others from natural consequences. It is important enough to say again: Be careful who your friends are, especially if managing your money is one of your goals.

Ask yourself the following questions when making a new friend:

- How often is a friend around when you don't have any money?
- How often does a friend pay for themselves when the two of you are together?
- How often do they ask you to pay for them?
- Do they ever offer to pay for you?

- Ask yourself the above questions about ten times for each potential friend.

Talk to your support team about the answers, and then decide if you want to keep someone as a friend. A reason I was able to lend or give money to a friend was I had a job and my life was (and still is) God-centered.

Before I help someone financially, I see if they have asked every government agency and religious organization to help them financially before I will consider helping them. If they didn't ask, I'd tell them to ask all of them first. If all the agencies said "No," I'd find out why they said no. Depending on their reasons for saying no and how many times they've asked for my help in the past, and depending on why they are asking for the money helps me decide if and how I'd help them!

By now you may realize that the world revolves around money. You have to give money to a business to receive a service or product. For example, you give money to the bus company to receive a bus ride or a bus pass. Nothing is free.

TO THE CHOICE MAKER:

- Do you see how the way you live and who your friends are protect or endanger your finances?
- What would happen if your money was stolen?
- What will you do if your hobbies cost more than you can afford?
- How important is it *to you* to pay for a place to live, electricity, one phone, transportation, and food if and when your food stamps run out for the month?

Ask questions like:

- How much money do I get a month?
- What are my required bills?
- How much does each bill cost?
- How much money is left after my required bills are paid?

The remaining money is yours to spend, save and/or give. Even if you choose to add a second phone, cable/dish, etc., they're not required bills; but if you buy those services, they become required bills. You must pay it and it reduces your spending money.

TO SUPPORT TEAM: Always listen to the choice maker's frustrations. Tell them your own money mistakes and the consequences you suffered. If you let the choice maker know what mistakes you made with your own money, they'd probably be more likely to accept and respect assistance.

An example, the choice maker might take some of your ideas, think about other ideas, and ignore some of your ideas. Instead of telling them something is too expensive, take them to the store, shop around for that item such as a cell phone with the understanding that the two of you are shopping and *not* buying anything *at this time*, but **maybe** at a later time. Have them show you the product or service they are interested in, and you show them the prices. Have the salesperson talk to *both of you* and explain all the possible monthly plans. When the two of you **leave**, ask and answer each other's questions.

Your goal: Find out how much they knew before going to the store and what they learned after going to the store! This rule should apply no matter what the topic is. They might be better prepared next time they go shopping. It is the same process for every new thing you purchase. This process could also be used to research information.

TO BOTH OF YOU: If you, the choice maker, has gotten into trouble with gambling, credit cards, etc., there are support groups and classes in the community to teach or re-teach money management skills. If you have a disability, be aware that classes may go at a fast pace. Support groups can also be helpful. Regaining control of money and *patiently* continuing to learn may be the answer. If you have trouble with checks, checking accounts, credit cards and/or buying things over the internet, consider paying your bills with money orders, *and avoid* credit cards and buying things online!

Chapter 6

Local Transportation

If you are low on money or want to exercise, you can walk, run, or ride a bike. There are three other possible ways to get around town faster:

A) Disability van
B) City bus
C) Driving

Disability Van

The disability van is one kind of public transportation. The only people allowed to ride the disability van are people who are eligible to ride, and the eligible person's caregiver and friend.

You must fill out paperwork to find out if you can ride the disability van. The transportation agency will send you a letter telling you if you are eligible. You have the right to have someone represent you or be at your side if you disagree with their decision.

Riding the van is much slower than riding the bus or driving! The people who schedule the rides make too many rides because they don't hire enough drivers and don't have enough vans. The van is very safe. If you are physically challenged and can easily break a bone by falling or if you get easily confused, the van is the safest option because the driver takes people to the door so riders never get lost!

One of the reasons the van is my least favorite transportation is, I've been dropped off so early the doors were still locked. I would wait alone and at times that was frightening. Being dropped off late was just as bad when I was going to school, work, or doctor's appointment.

The third problem I've had is waiting up to 30 minutes or longer for them to pick me up. I learned to deal with waiting by bringing things to do. I used my time wisely by calling doctor's offices, making more van rides, doing my homework, etc., so when I got home, I could spend my time doing what I wanted.

The van rules are different in every city and every state. In my city, this is how you go about setting up a ride. You or the caregiver need to call and schedule a ride 2-7 days in advance. The schedulers need to have your ID, the exact address of where you are going, the time you want to be picked up, and the exact time you need to be there if you have an appointment. You have to give them 75-90 minutes to get there on time! If you live on your own, you must schedule your own van rides!

Riding the City Bus

The city bus is another kind of public transportation. A lot of people without disabilities ride the bus for many reasons. Here are some of the reasons:

- Driving is expensive
- They lost their driver's license
- It's good for the environment

Different types of people ride the city bus. They include:

- People of different social and economic backgrounds
- People of different educational and professional backgrounds
- People of different races
- People of different ages
- People of different genders
- People of different religious and political backgrounds
- People with and without disabilities
- People who live on the street

You need to know how to keep yourself safe when you ride the city bus! Here are some ideas:

1) Be aware of who and what is around you.
2) Know the bus routes you need to take.
3) Do not make eye contact or talk to other passengers until you know how to ask for help safely.
4) Be aware of the people around you; their clothes, height, weight, and everything identifying.
5) If you see or hear trouble, report it to a worker.
6) When you are learning who is safe to talk to on the bus, only talk to people you trust from your place of worship, work or school. As you learn, you can talk to more people on the bus.

When I moved out of my parents' house and rented a room, the first thing I did was ride every city bus multiple times. I did this because I didn't know the streets well enough to understand the bus schedules and maps. At that time, I had no extra responsibilities, but I had a lot of trouble reading maps. In my opinion, my social experience was scary and strange. Since I was so sheltered growing up, I did not know how to tell if someone was safe.

TO THE CHOICE MAKER: Do you want to learn or relearn how to ride the city bus? What will you do if they change the bus routes?

1) If you are eligible, ride the disability van until you learn how to get to your destination. If the route changes, go back to the van until you learn the bus route to another destination. For example, you might only know the bus route to get to work. Take the bus to and from work, and ride the van everywhere else until you know how to get somewhere else; then take the bus there also, then repeat for each new place you go.
2) Ask another co-worker which bus you need to take.

3) Find out if the place you are going is on the street the bus drops you off on or if you have to walk a block or more.
4) Ask the driver to tell you when they get to your stop. If you have to walk a few blocks, ask the driver to point you in the correct direction!
5) If you continue to have trouble learning the buses and you still want to learn to ride, ask the bus company for special training!
6) Your support team can help you practice everything the bus company teaches you!
7) Tell the bus company what your transportation needs are by going to transportation meetings and by writing, calling, and emailing the administrators of the company. The administrators have control over the bus routes and money. If we never tell them our transportation needs, they will spend the money how they *think* it will best serve us, instead of how it <u>*really helps us*</u>!
8) Have someone ride with you wherever you go.
9) Finally, if you have tried everything to learn to ride the city bus and you still can't ride independently, I strongly recommend taking the disability van. However, it is ultimately your choice.

TO SUPPORT TEAM: The choice maker should slowly build his/her bus knowledge and apply the knowledge while riding the city bus and then gain more knowledge and apply that knowledge and repeat the process until you feel that the choice maker can ride the city bus alone.

TO THE BOTH OF YOU: *Everyone needs to learn to protect himself/herself just in case someone tries to hurt them.* You can protect yourself by using your voice, hands, pepper spray, a cell phone, etc. in an emergency. Make sure you understand each other's boundaries so you can work together as a team! You must know what each other's needs and wants are so you can understand and communicate with each other.

Driving

Driving is the fastest way to get around! Driving is the only thing I still wanted to do that my parents still didn't approve of! When I entered the 10th grade, I signed up for driver's education. After it was too late to drop classes, I had a seizure in class and the school pulled me out of driver's education and put me in study hall. I was so mad at both my parents and the school because they knew I had seizures.

I begged my mom to never tell the school about my seizures! My seizures were *mild*! The **only time** I ever blacked out was when I got very sick in the 3rd grade for seven days straight. However, I thought I could safely drive because I could feel my seizures coming on, I could carry on a conversation while I was having a seizure and had full use of the right side of my body while I was having a seizure, so I was able to pull over and stop.

As of March 2011, only 30% of me still wanted to drive. Why? As of 2013, I only wanted to drive 5% of the time. Because of some personal reasons, I was almost in a horrible car accident that I would not have been able to prevent. The other driver would have been at fault, but my driver was able to avoid it! Financially, I began to grasp how expensive it is to keep and maintain a car. In February and March of 2011, I had three seizures that I remember having ***after*** the seizure was over. However, I did feel it coming on!

For people who have physical limitations, there are accommodations for driving. My parents were still against me driving. My dad believed in doing things the normal way and if it could **not** be done the normal way, it should **not** be done at all. When I was 18 years old, my dad let me drive the truck in a field, and I ran into a bale of hay. In my defense, I had no idea what the rules of the road were. I hadn't studied the driver's guide. The only thing I knew about driving is what I saw my parents doing.

When I was 25 or 26, my doctor gave me permission to learn to drive. Even though I was 7-8 years older and I had ***my*** doctor's permission, my parents were still holding onto the bale of hay situation. They continued to hold that against me. When I told my parents that I did tell the doctor about being able to feel my seizures coming on, they said, "That doctor must be a pretty stupid doctor to give you permission to drive." I got a new doctor to say it was okay for me to drive. Why? My old doctor wasn't my doctor any longer.

I had four learner's permits. While I had my learner's permits, the Department of Vocational Rehabilitation said they would pay for me to learn to drive if: I got a driver's license, bought a vehicle, got insurance, and could pay to fix the vehicle when it breaks down.

The reason the Department of Vocational Rehabilitation was willing to pay for my driver's education was people who can drive and who have a car have a better chance of finding a job. What frustrated me most was there was nothing I could do to show my parents that I would be a better driver than I was 7-8 years ago. I thought they should at least tell me what I needed to do to *earn their trust* with their car!

Mom was quietly against it. Dad said, "No!" The more he told me I could not do it, the more I wanted to drive!

My college classes required attending live shows. I tried taking the disability van. Sometimes, I would get there too early or too late. Sometimes, I had to wait for the disability van outside in the dark in the middle of downtown.

Although I never had a safe place to practice driving and my father was against it, I still wanted to learn. Finally, what helped me realize I could not drive was a man named Eli. He let me try to steer his pedal car. It had four seats. He let me drive the pedal car, so if I had trouble steering, he could keep it on the road, and there would be less chance of crashing.

TO THE CHOICE MAKER: The reason I shared this goal and dream is to show that nobody gets everything they want in life. Try hard to get as independent as you can.

TO SUPPORT TEAM: The reason it took me so long to realize that I could not drive is that my parents refused to let me find out for myself how safe or dangerous it would be. After my doctor gave me permission and I got my learner's permit, the Department of Vocational Rehabilitation said they would consider paying for my driver's education if I had a car and a *desire to get a job*! My parents had the ability to support me by letting me practice my driving lessons with *their* car.

Another reason I fought so hard for so long about my perceived right to drive is I had been told for so long that I couldn't do many things because I'm disabled. I found out I could do a lot with God's help! I proved to my parents that anything is possible! I now know driving isn't a right! If someone gets caught drinking and driving, they **should lose** their driver's license for life! If someone does something wrong because of their disability, they should be given chances and/or forced to take classes to accommodate their disability.

A lot of people resent being told "No" when they don't understand why they can't do something. Letting the person with a disability find out they can't do something helps them learn what their limitations are. This can sometimes help them to say no on their own and/or will teach them when to say no. Help them figure out their limitations (including financial) by asking them specific questions just like you would ask a child without disabilities!

If you make them part of the decision-making process, it will be easier for both of you in the long-run to get what you both need and want. This will help them gain the skills to make informed choices. The goal should be:

- To teach them when to stand up for themselves
- To know when to ask questions
- To know when to accept someone else's answer

Chapter 7

Learning a Job or a Career

A job or career is how people make money. However, the job must be learned before the work can be done.

College helps people get a higher paying job.

A relative, friend, or someone you know can teach you how to do a job.

Sometimes, the boss can also teach people what they want them to know and/or how they want the job done. This is called on-the-job training or OJT.

There are also people who have a job coach job that can help them learn their job and/or help them keep their job.

School or College

I graduated from high school with a diploma. I took a one-year break from school, moved back to the city, and started college. When I started college, I had to take remedial classes to get caught up to college level. Below college level means classes below the 100 level.

The first two years of college can be done at a community college, which is cheaper than a four-year college.

Sometimes, I took breaks in between college quarters for different reasons. Some good reasons to take a temporary break from school is:

- If college is causing you to have physical, mental, or emotional problems, finish the quarter or semester then take a break before going back! Your health is more important than a college degree!
- Family emergency
- Financial difficulties

When a person goes to college, they are being trained to do a job that will pay more money in the future. There are a lot of jobs that require a college degree. If you want to go to college before you decide what lifetime career you want, take all the required classes for an Associate Degree. Once you know what you want to do, you can start taking the classes for that career.

Only take classes that the school counselor says you need and choose elective classes you want to take. Don't take college classes or get a degree that someone else wants you to. Take what you need and want! You *might* want a job you don't like so you can earn more money.

My College Choices

My first choice was taking the Early Childhood Education program. I chose this because I had been a teacher's aide for a semester, and the following year I was a Sunday school teacher's aide for a Sunday school class.

While I was in class at school, the teacher handed me a pair of latex gloves. I started to put them on using my teeth. He said I couldn't use my teeth. I explained my disability. After a few more talks, they took me out of my classes and the program. It was explained that state law requires that *all* childcare workers must wear gloves.

I was frustrated and I didn't know what I wanted to do, so I dropped out of school for a few years. I didn't want to do anything education or employment-wise, but I stayed busy! I finally decided I wanted to be a voice teacher. As I started my studies in music, I found out that I had to be able to play one other instrument besides my voice.

After taking a few classes, I chose to drop out because most instruments require two hands. I thought it would be unfair to my students because I had to play an instrument with one hand

and my students needed to learn to play correctly, with two hands!

Next, I started listening to people with mental health issues and intellectual disabilities. Most of them seemed very unhappy to have a guardian, protective payee, and/or a caregiver because they wanted do things their guardian, protective payee, and/or caregiver would **not** let them do.

Later, I joined a Bible Study with people who had severe intellectual disabilities. Most of these people were unable to talk, unable to use their hands, and/or unable to walk. However, they all had smiles on their faces and loved Jesus Christ. This made that group of people wonderful to be around. After two years of knowing them, I started hanging out with some of them outside the Bible Study.

This was hard on me because the people working in the helping profession overprotected them! From what I witnessed at the time, residential caregiving agencies guarded their clients from anyone who was not a professional or family member. It seems reasonable to me to do a police background check on everyone who wanted to be their friend and everyone the choice maker chose as friends. Another type of overprotecting is protecting people from doing things that are age appropriate.

When I found out that the problem of overprotecting and not listening to the people who have mental health issues and intellectual disabilities was a system-wide problem, not an agency problem, and that every agency seemed to be unable to change their policies to be more client friendly, I chose to go back to college and get my Associate Degree in social work! A social worker can work with many different kinds of people. For example, they can work with the elderly, children, people who have mental health issues or intellectual disabilities, etc.

Over the years, many people with intellectual disabilities have asked me to help them do different things or they tell me, "My guardian won't let me _____ (fill in the blank)." I have continued to listen and ask questions like:

- Why do you want to do that?
- Why won't they let you?

I chose to write this book so I'd be able to help more people and teach them to do the things they were asking me to help them do. With this book and the workbook I wrote, I can put a class together to teach people the skills they need to learn so they can do the things they want to do.

TO THE CHOICE MAKER:

How to decide if you want to go to college: There are jobs out there that require more education than a high school diploma or GED. Required classes are classes you have to take to get the degree you need to get the career you want. There are jobs that don't require going to college, but those jobs pay less money!

Therefore, if you want to earn more money, go to college!

Another reason to go to college is for personal reasons. These classes teach you things that have nothing to do with getting a job. Personal enrichment classes might include budgeting your money, how to be a good parent, etc. If you want to go to college, you need to think about the cost. Financial aid pays for classes that will help you get a job or career, but they won't pay for personal enrichment classes.

The very first time I went to college the Department of Vocational Rehabilitation paid for my college classes. The next couple of years my parents paid for it. When I chose to get my social work degree, I got a Pell grant because my dad retired, and he was old enough to choose to work part-time. Pell grants, loans, work studies, practicum, and/or scholarships are different ways to pay for college. Scholarships are earned, but financial aid gives you a scholarship.

How to choose a college degree:
- What do you like to do? Name as many job options as you can think of that you are good at and that you would enjoy doing.

- Do you want to make any of your hobbies a job?

TO SUPPORT TEAM: If your choice maker will let you, help them choose if college is right for them, and help them find out what they are good at and enjoy to help them get the most enjoyable job they can find.

- Why do they want to go to college?
- Does the job they want require a college degree?
- What are their options for paying for college?

If they want to go to college and they can't afford it, help them work out a way to pay for it. Possible plans could be:

- Part-time job
- Full-time job
- Pell grant
- Work Study
- Scholarship
- Family
- Practicum

Chapter 8

Employment

When I was in elementary school, I dreamed of being a teacher for young children around 2nd or 3rd grade. As I got older, my dream job changed.

I remember wanting to go to a different country and preach the Gospel of Jesus Christ. I never left the United States. Part of the reason was I needed to take a job skill to the country such as teaching English, giving medical care, etc. I had no skills at the time along with struggling with my physical and learning disabilities.

Later, I wanted to be a lawyer to help people with disabilities. I finally realized that being a lawyer would be too stressful and unhealthy for me. The reason I felt that way is because when my stress level is high, I get anxious and/or panicky. My stomach hurts. I also get sweaty. I have acid reflux and I don't enjoy feeling sick. I refuse to work a job that will cause my health problems to increase on a daily basis.

I need a career that will keep me healthy!

I have done volunteer work at a nursing home where my grandfather was living. I decided I would never work in a nursing home! The only way I would ever volunteer again is if my parents had to live there.

I have had the Department of Vocational Rehabilitation (DVR) place me in sheltered employment three times, but most sheltered employment jobs required using both hands and the use of individual fingers. I only have use of my fingers on my right hand, but I have no use on my left hand! DVR placed me there to assess my job readiness skills to figure out what I was good at. I always went prepared for a telephone job.

Phone jobs require answering the phone, stuffing envelopes, typing, greeting people, etc. My only problem with that kind of job was that every time they got new software on the computer,

I'd have to learn a new computer program over and over again! The last time DVR worked with me I got a minimum wage telephone job as a market researcher. I had that job for 1½ years.

I currently want to be a teacher and an advocate for people with intellectual disabilities, but I'd advocate for people with other disabilities too. (At this time, I volunteer.) To me, how a person with any kind of disability thinks is equally as important as their health! I want to teach people with disabilities to make educated decisions. I want to teach them how and why certain things will help them be healthy, and how some things are unhealthy!

People usually find a job that makes them enough money to pay their bills and to have enough money to have some fun in life, and other people like to earn more money to save for retirement or to give to a non-profit organization. Most places of worship are non-profit.

Some jobs pay more in the same business. How? Some employers pay employees more by seniority. The most common way to make more money in the company is to get a promotion. This is done by applying for jobs usually inside the company when there's a job opening. Only apply for jobs that you have the skills to do. Why do some jobs pay more than other jobs? Higher paying positions have more responsibilities! The higher the position, the more responsibilities there are!

The way to get a higher position in a company is to learn the company's language and the language in a field. Company language is language that is used at a specific company. Each company has its own language.

Another way to get the job you want to do for the rest of your life is to take any job you can find to pay your bills and save money for college. When you graduate from college, you can get the job of your dreams!

Don't Be Afraid to Make a Mistake!

Wisdom comes through the experience of making mistakes, having successes and taking responsibility for both! The reason for taking responsibility for both your mistakes and your successes is to learn from your mistakes. Mistakes help you to know what to avoid so you make fewer mistakes and you know what you did right. You'll feel great when you succeed!

Communicate with people at work. Most people know how to do this. If you struggle with communicating with your co-workers or boss, tell your job coach! Do you struggle with the difference between personal and professional relationships? Do you struggle with setting boundaries at work? If yes, tell your support team.

What is the difference between a career and a job? A career is a job you want to do until you retire. A job is a place you work until you can find another job. For example, I was a market researcher. I did that job until I needed more time to write my books. Another example is the person who wants to be a caregiver until they retire; they chose to make caregiving their career. For the person who is a caregiver until they finish college or until they find a higher paying job, caregiving is just a job—a way to earn money.

My career goal is to teach people with intellectual disabilities to be their own best advocate, how to set boundaries, how to make choices, and how to stick to the choices they made! Being a social worker is a step toward my goal of being a teacher and an advocate for people with disabilities. Here's how to choose the career you want. You start by asking yourself two kinds of questions.

The first kind of question is, "What are you good at?" Be honest with yourself! Nobody is good at everything!

- Are you good with machines? If so, what kinds of machines?
- Are you good at doing physical labor?

- Are you good at office work? If so, how many words can you accurately type a minute?
- Are you good at restaurant work?
- Are you good at working with the public?
- Are you good at working around and with co-workers?
- Are you good working by yourself?
- Are you good at fixing computers when they are broken or crash?
- Are you good working with animals?
- Are you good with plants?
- Are you good with planes?
- Are you good at writing?

The second kind of questions is, "What do you ENJOY doing?"

- Do you enjoy working with machines? If so, what kinds of machines?
- Do you enjoy doing physical labor?
- Do you enjoy office work? If so, how many words can you accurately type a minute?
- Do you enjoy doing restaurant work?
- Do you enjoy working with the public?
- Do you enjoy working around and with your co-workers?
- Do you enjoy working by yourself?
- Do you enjoy fixing computers when they are broken or crash?
- Do you enjoy typing on a computer and getting into different computer programs? If so, how many words can you accurately type a minute?
- Do you enjoy working with animals?
- Do you enjoy working with plants?
- Do you enjoy working with planes?
- Do you enjoy writing?

By doing what you are good at and what you enjoy, you will like going to work every day! Some jobs don't pay very much, but those jobs are enjoyable. For example, a person in a music career or a career in a religious organization might be a low paying job. Religious jobs could be working at your place of worship, working in a religious school, etc. The benefit of working in such a place is that everyone shares your spiritual values. Some people just need to make a lot of money and don't care if their job is enjoyable. Their reward is money! Other people like to earn extra money so they have enough money to give to religious, social, or non-profit organizations.

The more you know about yourself, the easier it will be to find the best match for a job or career that you will have time for, you will be able to enjoy and you will be good at!

Know yourself: How long are you able to work? Before you look for a job answer the following questions:

- How many hours can you work before you get tired?
- How many hours a day do you want to work?
- Do you need to work part-time?
- Can you work full-time?
- If you can only work part-time, how many hours are you able to work a day?
- If part-time, how many days a week?
- If you are looking for part-time work, will you take morning, afternoon, or evenings, or any shift they want or does the shift not matter?
- What days of the week are you willing to work?
- Will you work any day of the week the boss asks you to?
- Will you work any hour that the boss asks you to?
- Are you willing to work weekends?
- Do you have a religion that believes it is wrong to work on a certain day of the week?
- Will you work on your days off, if asked?
- Can you work rotating shifts?

If you can't do something, when you apply for a job write it on the application, and while you are being interviewed tell the interviewer right away, not after you are hired. The boss hires people based on *their needs*. If they hire you, they assume you CAN do the job. If you need any accommodations to complete the job, they need to know before they hire you.

Gaining More Independence

Once you have a job and can pay all your required bills, you'll know how much money you have to spend and save. What you spend the rest of the money on is your choice.

The kind of services people usually think about buying are going out to eat, getting cable TV, living alone, buying a house instead of renting, buying a car or truck, etc. The types of products people think about buying are new video games, a new TV, a cell phone, etc.

*Talk to your support team before giving any organization money! If they have never seen or heard of someone or a company and/or if they disapprove, don't give money to that organization! Find organizations they have heard of!

Chapter 9

The Challenges of Living on Your Own

Here are some terms:

- Support group: Place you go to help you stop an addiction such as smoking, drinking, drugs, or gambling, etc. It could also be a place you go to help you cope and deal with a disability or a family member's disability.
- Support network: Includes *all* the people that you have around you. It's important to know who you call for help for what you need. It is also important to let others know when you can be the extra help.

After I graduated in 1990, I spent a couple of months living with my parents, and I started singing in the church choir. One of the choir ladies offered me room and board at her house. This was how I moved into the community. This lady and her husband were politically active and that is how I got started in politics.

While I was living there, my parents thought they were taking advantage of me politically. I made phone calls for the Republican Action Club. I guess my parents thought I didn't want to do this, and thought those people scared me, or that they were telling me how to vote.

During the 11 months I lived with this family, there were things I did around the house. I was also learning how to ride the city buses and became eligible to ride the disability van. Even though I was involved in ministry and had governmental assistance, something was still missing. Church and these agencies were not meeting my social needs.

When I moved into my own apartment, I had no idea how to schedule my days and I was bored. Six months after moving out on my own, I had a nervous breakdown and ended up in a mental health hospital for 14 days. By going to the hospital, I started learning how to plan my days, choose friends, and set boundaries.

A disability agency helped me realize that, because of my physical limitations and my learning disability, I needed someone to come to my home and help me if I was going to live alone. They got an agency to help me with what I was unable to do. The following is a partial list of things this kind of agency can do to help people with disabilities. They can help with cooking, cleaning, and personal care task needs! This is a partial list of personal care tasks. They include assistance with bathing, toileting, brushing hair, brushing teeth, help with medication, getting dressed, transferring clients in and out of bed and wheelchair, etc. If this is something you need, talk to your support team to find out what it is.

One of my first supports I developed was the Evergreen Club. The Evergreen Club was a place where people who have mental health issues go. At the time I went there, it was a day program that helped mental health clients maintain their social life and helped them get jobs. My reason for going to the Evergreen Club was for social and emotional support while learning how to structure my day!

At that time, I wanted to take care of my grandfather who had Alzheimer's disease so he would be taken care of by family. Other family members chose to put him in a nursing home, and I chose to spend my time visiting him in the nursing home until he died.

The clients at the Evergreen Club quickly found out that I had a healthy spiritual background and that I knew how to work with the political system. They found out that I talked to elected officials. The people with mental health disabilities would come and ask me the same things that people with intellectual disabilities ask me, but they'd also say things like, "I do not want to go into the hospital" or "I do not want to live in a group home" or "I want to live in a group home or hospital."

I was young and had very strong values. My values included honesty, responsibility, and communication. A lot of the clients were asking me for help instead of asking the professionals. In a way, I kind of became a political and religious caseworker.

Politically, I gave them the information they asked for. Religiously, I would only give them information if they let me share my faith with them. I wanted them to understand and apply their faith to their own life.

*I got frustrated and burned out from the Mental Health system after three years at the Evergreen Club. My caseworker would not help me while the professionals were shoving help down the throats of people who didn't want help.

In fact, I was very, very tired because these people came to me for my political knowledge, but they would not follow through with what I told them. At that time in my life, I didn't understand why the professionals kept those clients on their caseload when they refused to accept or cooperate with them. Back then, if it were me, I'd walk away from someone who let me know they didn't want my help. To me, the professionals were wasting their time and the taxpayers' money; and here I was a willing client who would accept and cooperate with any professional help they would give me. They didn't help me!

It didn't bother me to give my peers political advice along with sharing my faith with them. What I hated was when someone wasted my time that I could have spent doing something I wanted to do or helping someone who would accept my help by trying to do what I told them to.

That year, I also started going to college full-time. I became friends with a person who was violently mentally ill. I also volunteered my time at a Christian homeless shelter.

TO THE CHOICE MAKER: Even with my boundaries, I still made a bad choice in choosing a friend. This shows you how setting boundaries will help you make fewer bad choices!

Back to my life story. I chose to be this person's friend for a couple of reasons. I was bored, and this person didn't smoke, drink alcohol or use *illegal* drugs. I guess I believed because it's his disability and because it wasn't caused by bad habits **and** he had no control over his temper, I treated it like a disability. I didn't realize his anger was equally as dangerous as the person who drinks and/or uses *illegal* drugs.

As you can see, even though this was a bad choice for a friend, **_I learned from my mistake!_** I also remember the good things he taught me and learned from them. Just because he was a bad choice for a friend does not mean he was stupid. In fact, he was very intelligent!

On one hand, if people would have let me make my choices when I was growing up, I probably would have had an easier time listening to what other friends thought about him. Since I refused to listen, this is one area I had to learn from my mistake!

However, he never hit me and he never touched me in inappropriate ways! He never lived with me, and he never even asked to live with me, probably because he knew if he did ask, I would say, "NO!" and tell my dad.

The trouble started when I wanted to watch a TV program or do my homework and he wanted my attention. He was bored and just wanted me all to himself, even though I had other things to do. I had set up some boundaries for my college schedule, my homework, and most importantly, me!

Remember I wrote about my birthmark on the right side of my face? I guess people in the community, including the law enforcement were asking him, "Did you hit her?" *Nobody ever asked me*! I thought his behavior was getting crazier because he was getting accused of beating me up. I thought I had to do something so he would calm down, but I didn't know who to talk to, so that the law enforcement would know it's a birthmark and *not* a bruise!

I remember hearing about a surgery that could remove birthmarks. Toward the end of the year I decided that I would go through seven of these surgeries. My thinking was, 'If I remove my birthmark, he will be calmer because people will stop accusing him of beating me.'

The next year was my second year at the Evergreen Club. One friend, who had been in denial of her mental illness for 20 years, kept getting help she rejected. She refused to cooperate with the professionals who insisted on helping her. All this time, I was not getting the help I needed and would have cooperated with the professionals if they would have assisted with my physical limitations too.

I went back to being politically active with the Republicans for my physical safety. When I felt safe, I went back to being a disability advocate! Just because people are entitled to something does not mean the entitlement should be shoved down their throat. Each client should be allowed to accept or reject every entitlement that is offered to them unless rejecting it endangers someone else's health!

I have compassion for people who smoke, drink alcohol and/or do *illegal* drugs, but I still have my personal boundaries. I might choose to be around someone who chooses to do bad habits, but that's my choice! I support anyone who wants to stop bad habits! However, no one should be forced to stop, only encouraged!

For three years, I watched people go in and out of a mental health hospital. Some people liked getting the help and others hated it. I saw clients stay in denial of their disability, and I watched the system continue to try to help people who never realized that they needed help. It was like watching someone addicted to drugs who keeps denying that they have a problem. To me, it might be worth the money to help people who can't see their need for help for five years, but if they still can't see their need for professional help, they should have their case closed until the client seeks professional help again in the future.

Help the people who have a mental illness, who take their medications as prescribed by the doctor, and do all the right things and still need help. If someone admits to having mental health issues and is smart enough *to know* when to ask for help, there should be money available to those people when the symptoms of their disability show up! It is flat wrong not to!

Help the people who need it, want it, or put the public in danger because of their disability! If they are a danger to the public and are refusing help, they *must* get the help or go to jail or prison if they break the law like any other person without disabilities! If there is any money left, help people who need it, but can't see their need, and will accept help. Don't help people who reject help!

In 1994, I started attending a Tuesday night group with people who were severely physically challenged. Most of these new friends were unable to walk, talk, or use their hands; however, they were very happy! This was two hours, one night a week, and I really enjoyed myself! These people had no questions or demands! It was a place I could relax and regain my energy!

Soon after I started this group, I had to get a no contact order against that angry man. A no contact order is a legal piece of paper a person gets from the courthouse so that the police know that one person is having problems with another person whose name is written on the paper. ***To get a protection order, someone must have threatened your safety.*** Both the victim and the person causing the problem have their names on the protection order.

There are other legal names for these legal papers. If you need protection, your support network or the courthouse can help you figure out which legal document you need. The names of the two people are written on that legal document. The police will never know that one specific person is threatening another person unless there are legal papers showing there's a problem. Without legal papers, the police will never know that there's a problem. *Unless a person's life is in danger at the time they call*, an officer can't help you. That's why legal papers are so crucial! I wanted this person to stay away from me!

As I continued my surgeries, I started talking to a lot of volunteers on the phone that worked for a disability agency. The phone felt safe because that dangerous person kept breaking the law by trying to contact me even with the protection order against him.

One volunteer encouraged me to get a music degree since I already loved to sing and sang in the choir. I wanted to be a voice teacher. To become a voice teacher, I had to go to a lot of concerts that most people dislike. The concerts were instrumental or the singing was in foreign languages. I did not know anyone who wanted to attend the concerts with me, so my dad wanted me to ask the volunteer who encouraged me to get a music degree. My dad was too tired to go out at night because he worked full-time, didn't like this music, and hated driving downtown.

In 1995, I stopped my surgeries. I chose to set a goal and respect my dad's wishes. I asked this person if we could be friends outside work where I was the client and he was the professional. He had no choice! He had to say no and that made me mad!

I asked him if he would personally want to be my friend *if* the rule wasn't there. He said, "Yes," if the rules would let him. That's the reason I felt it was worth fighting for. So, I set a new goal! I chose to fight to change that rule! Everyone should be able to choose their friends no matter what their job is. People are people and should be able to be friends with anyone they want including clients and/or employees.

There are good and bad people everywhere, including religious people! There are good and bad people in every job. To protect clients, students, residents, etc., this made no sense to me.

The thing that mattered to me was, it should be everyone's individual choice to say yes or no when they are asked! My dad was supporting me by giving me the money to make the long-distance phone calls and gave me moral support! After 1½ years, I stopped trying.

In 1995, I also had to get my second no contact order and chose to continue school. When I realized I couldn't play an instrument and sing at the same time, I quit college again!

The clients were harassing me and crossing *my* boundaries. The professionals refused to help me, so to protect my sanity I left! I decided if the professionals would not enforce consequences when there was inappropriate behavior then I'd be happier and safer not attending the Evergreen Club.

In 1996, I became more socially involved with my "group friends." Even though they had severe disabilities, I appreciated how happy they were, and that they made my life enjoyable!

I had another goal: To get a lady elected to office. I volunteered by calling registered voters! After I tried to get this person elected to office, I got a job for 1½ years as a market researcher. (I wrote about my employment life in an earlier chapter.) As you can see, hobbies, interests, goals, and support networks can change over time!

TO THE CHOICE MAKER: If you choose to move out and live with roommates, here's a safe way to do it.

- *Know yourself!*
- *Know your likes and dislikes!*

If you don't clearly distinguish what you like and don't like, you might go for anything. When you know your likes and dislikes:

- Communicate them!

You can speak, write, draw, or use a combination of ways to communicate! If you are unable to communicate clearly, your support team might worry about you. When something is very important to you, others might not recognize your expressed needs and wants, and you might be ignored!

- Make your home safe!

Setting boundaries! Your boundaries show others who you are by what you stand for! Set boundaries to protect your:

- Body. One example of protecting your body is telling someone, "Don't hit me!" Another is example is, "Don't call me before 7:00 am or after 9:00 pm; I need my sleep!"

- Feelings and Emotions. This is an example of how to set a boundary if someone is hurting your feelings, "If you call me that name, I will _____ (fill in the blank)!" Whatever you put in the blank, you must follow through every time that person calls you that. When you do the same thing every time, people will know you are serious! If you change your response to the same action, they won't take you seriously and will keep calling you names.
- Mind. This is what I mean by protecting my mind. If someone is asking me for help, I will think of every possible solution to help them. I'll do this a couple of times. If they never take the information, I won't help them in the future. If the person takes some of the information I've given them, I will help them again if and when I have time!
- Time. An example of setting a time boundary is when someone calls on the phone and you have to say, "I only have ten minutes. My caregiver is coming at 9:30." Another kind of time boundary is when you start a job or college, you might need to tell your friends, "I can't go out tonight. I have to study for my test."
- Money. A money boundary might be, "I don't talk about money with friends" or "I'm not a bank, so I won't lend money."
- Property. There are two meanings that I know for the word property. The first is the land that a building sits on such as a house. There is also personal property, which could be anything you own.

   For example, I have the right to tell people *don't* smoke in my house. *You have the right to tell people how to treat your property!*

However, in order for people to respect your boundaries, you must tell them what your boundaries are. You have no right to get mad at anyone for violating a boundary if you never told them what the boundary is that they violated! People are only responsible for what they know!

You never have to explain why you set a boundary; however, it is smart to tell some people out of respect! For example, when I was single, I let a couple of my male friends hug me. When I got married, I changed that boundary. The men who knew me when I was single deserved to understand why I didn't want them to hug me. If they don't understand after I explain it, it's their issue. However, there's no reason to tell my new male friends.

I tell different people why I have certain boundaries. There's probably no one other than my husband who knows the reason behind every boundary I have.

My boundaries don't change, but how I explain my boundaries might change. Sometimes, I share the reasons behind my boundaries because I want to understand the reason for other people's boundaries. I tell family members when there's a reason they should know. Finally, I tell my professionals such as my doctors, counselor, etc. when I think they need to know.

When people know your boundaries and they break them, you have the responsibility to take action. If you don't, they might continue to violate your boundaries because you didn't give them any consequences.

Your action could be a reminder the first time they break them, and then make them face stronger consequences the next time. Handle it friend by friend and boundary by boundary! For example: My best friend will let me call anytime, day or night, but no one else is allowed to call him in the middle of the night.

- Plan your days (make time and write things down)!

Your plans need to include things that have to be done throughout the day. The kinds of things you have to plan in a day are your job/college classes, possibly homework, doctor's appointments, necessary errands such as grocery shopping, doing things for the kids, etc.

Write down what you do for fun. This includes going to parties, Bible Study, out on a date, or anything else that's fun or relaxing.

If you don't write down your daily plans, such as doctor appointments or plans to go out with a friend, you might make plans to do two things at the same time by accident!

Chapter 10

Contact People

How do you contact people?

- Telephone
- E-mail
- Text
- Snail mail
- In person
- Social media

Who do you contact?

- Friends
- Businesses
- Family

You might wonder when you will have time to call, text, or e-mail people. It's called multitasking. I personally choose to make personal calls when I'm on the bus/van because I want to keep my personal life private! I have used it for business calls while I was waiting for the bus/van or on the bus/van. I've scheduled my paratransit rides because I can't always do my homework on a moving vehicle. You need to schedule time to cook, eat, and have fun. These three things can be done while doing other things.

*All these things have to be taken into consideration when planning out your 7-day week!

*If you choose to live on your own, you will be 100% responsible for everything!

If you need help, that's fine. There are agencies that send caregivers out to people's homes who have disabilities, but they can't be there 24 hours a day, seven days a week. If you want more information, call 211. I will write about these agencies in a later chapter.

Making Friends

Where? The places you go to the most:
- Place of worship
- Religious organizations
- Political organization(s)
- Place of employment
- College
- Places of shared goals, interests or hobbies
- Online

Before I go any further, there are three things you should know:
- Don't try to be friends with everybody.
- If you try, you will have no "me time" for yourself.
- If you try, you won't have quality time with any friends.

Looking for friends who have two or more things in common is a smart idea.

I have friends who are Christians and who have disabilities and/or are disability advocates. I have a friend that is one of the leaders of the church where I have taught about disabilities and accommodations. This leader has a relative who has become disabled since I first met him.

You can also look for friends by looking at their personality. For example, some people like softer voices. Other people are hard of hearing and may need others to speak loudly. Other personality traits could be honest/dishonest, bold/shy, etc. Also, there are people you *need to avoid*, and others that you should avoid.

We need to avoid people who will cause us harm. This could be people who always ask for money, hit you or threaten to hit you, knowingly hurt your feelings, or touch you in inappropriate places.

- Sexual harm: People who touch you in uncomfortable ways and/or sex offenders.

Parents and society protect children from sex offenders. There are places to find out who the sex offenders are living in your area, where you work or at school.

Avoid people who do things that cause _you_ health problems. We should avoid people who have lifestyle differences such as:

- Tobacco differences
- Alcohol differences
- Illegal drug differences
- Morality differences

There is nothing wrong with any of these groups being friends with each other, but a large part of this chapter has been about setting boundaries.

As a nonsmoker, my smoking friends are my telephone friends. I can multitask by talking to my smoking friends on the phone while I'm doing something else such as doing a search-a-word puzzle. I can't multitask by visiting my smoking friends at work. I either have to go do the things I need and want to do or go outside and visit around _all of the smokers_, not just my friend! My friends who smoke are strictly my phone friends and I go out with nonsmokers/ex-smokers. I have two smokers who are family members who I hang out with one or two times a year. I don't have time to build a new friendship. Be honest: If someone asks you to be your friend and you don't want to, give an honest reason or don't give them a reason at all!

Build friendships **slowly**!

- Get to know someone when other people are around
- Get to know someone one-on-one in public

Places that you can get to know someone one-on-one in

public would be:

- Restaurant
- Shopping mall

Any place where you can talk with each other around other people is a good place to get to know someone. If you think the person is safe, you can start to give them the following information, but not too quickly! The information is your:

- Phone number(s)
- E-mail address
- Social media information

The order doesn't matter. Don't give them all your information at the same time!

- Physical address (This should be *last*!)

The reason you want to give your physical address last is to keep yourself safe! Finally, if you have any problems in setting or keeping boundaries, ask your support team for help!

TO SUPPORT TEAM: Help your person with a disability figure out what their likes and dislikes are. This helps them know themselves better!

If they ask for help, help them set their <u>own</u> boundaries! If they don't ask, don't help them, but you should still share your history about *why and how* you set your boundaries! Examples of this would be telling them about your personal mistakes and personal successes. Tell them about books you have read to get your wisdom.

Respect them by telling them:

- When they want to do something that is harmful.

For example, if the choice maker will die from foods that they eat, then they <u>can't</u> learn from this mistake! Another health issue, there are things that can make disabilities worse, like drinking alcohol. My personal opinion: When it is health related, tell them to talk to their doctor. When it is medicine related, have them talk to their doctor and pharmacist!

- Respect their boundaries, even when you don't agree with them because they are unsafe!

Allow them to express themselves to you and let them practice telling you their different opinions and boundaries. You can give them different responses so they can practice being firm with their boundaries. Practice makes perfect!

TO THE BOTH OF YOU: There is a program to help people with disabilities pay their bills if the person never learns to pay their own bills. It is called representative protective payee. If you have trouble with money, having a payee might make it possible to live on your own!

There is also another kind of program that will send a caregiver over to help you do things like bathing, filing your nails, brushing your hair or teeth, getting in or out of bed, etc. and housework that you are unable to do because of your disabilities! They do housework and personal care tasks that you are unable to do because of your disability or disabilities! The name of the program is different in every state. If you are interested, ask your case manager about getting a caregiver in your home.

If you are unable to do personal care tasks or housework, you *can* still live alone!

TO THE CHOICE MAKER: If you are in programs or services you don't want that you are entitled to, explain this to your support team and tell them why you don't want these services.

As a person with disabilities, I'm asking you to ***please*** take care of your health. Go to your doctors' offices. You don't need more disabilities than you already have! Doctors may be able to help lessen the severity of your disabilities!

Chapter 11

Boundaries for Dating

It is your choice to be in a dating relationship. If you choose to be in a relationship, you should take the time to find someone you can talk with and that you like to be around! It is better to be alone than to have a relationship that makes you feel horrible. This chapter helps you choose your boundaries in a relationship.

In an earlier chapter, you chose *your* lifestyle; what kind of person you want to be! Let's say you chose to never smoke. In this chapter, the question is, is it okay if your friend, date, roommate, lover smokes?

When you make a choice about living together, dating, or marrying someone, there are a lot of things to consider. After reading through this chapter, it would be smart to talk to a few people you respect.

If you are a religious person, talk to the clergy at your place of worship, and other men and women you respect. Talk to men and women in all age groups: older, younger and the same age as you, and to your support team because people of different ages and genders think differently.

Sources include:

- Place of worship
- Family
- Friends
- Library
- TV
- Radio
- Newspaper
- Internet
- Support team

Each person must choose their personal boundaries for dating!

First, name all the possible places you can meet new people. This includes the mall, grocery store, school, and work. It also includes public transportation, place of worship, the bar, your hobby organizations, clubs, support groups, doctors' offices, etc.

Which places do you think are safe, unsafe, or neutral for meeting new friends, possible dates, or a lifetime partner?

If you are having trouble choosing, look at what most people who have your values do and say. Here is another way to see if these places are good, bad, or neutral places for making new friends. Ask yourself the following questions:

- Are you comfortable with the way most of the people behave at the place?
- Would you do and say what these people are doing or saying when you are with friends outside this place?
- Do most of the people there respect your physical, emotional, spiritual, social, and mental boundaries?
- If these people disrespect you, how do they disrespect you?
- Is the place bad or just a few of the people in that place?

These questions help **_you_** choose your boundaries! You need to know why your boundaries are what they are! The only reason for explaining your reasons behind any choice you make is that your support team might feel the need to protect you from being taken advantage of. When they know your likes and dislikes ahead of time, they might feel more comfortable! By your support team knowing the reasons for your boundaries, they can alert you if they see something you think is wrong!

If you can prove that you are making your own choices by explaining your reasons for how you made your choice, or why you need or want something and telling them why you want certain things, then you are well on your way! This includes proving to them no one talked you into doing or saying something you don't want!

It is important that you make choices based on *your* values, needs and wants, which can include other people's opinions.

However, you need to make choices by looking at many sources. For example, you could compare dating service prices!

A dating service is a business that helps people safely date others. Of course, they charge money—that's how they stay in business. It is important that you need or want a product or service you are paying for. It is important that what you do, how you behave and act, and what you say *follows your values*!

Chapter 12

Keeping Yourself Safe

Keep yourself safe by observing potential friends in public *before* getting together in private. You might want to know about their job, religion, hobbies, etc. (It depends on the kind of relationship you want.)

Finding out some of the information you want *takes time*! If you ask someone everything you want to know when you first meet them, they will either be scared off or will tell you what they think you want them to say!

For example, let's say someone you know won't date anyone who drinks and they want to date you. They *might* lie to you so you will go out on a date. If you were the one that drinks alcohol and knew they don't date people who drink, would you tell the truth? Maybe.

What do you want to know about new people you meet, especially someone you would consider dating or marrying?

- Do you want to know their hobbies, job, values including are they religious, or do you know what their bad habits are? We all have bad habits, including me.
- You find these things out by listening to them talk over time and by watching their behaviors and actions.
- What do they say and what do they do when you are not around?
- Finally, how long do you want to know them before making sure they are telling the truth?

What do other people say about them?

This is how I safely get to know people:

1) When I meet people face-to-face, I have to see them in public often, so I know if they are safe and if we have

enough things in common to make it worth my time and energy to be friends with them.
2) I listen to their tone of voice and body language. Body language includes looking them in the eye, and watching their feet and hands.
3) How do they treat other people? If they scare me, I'll avoid them.
4) I'd keep talking to them at the public place where we met.
5) If we both decide we like each other as friends, I'll ask if they want to exchange phone numbers.

The telephone is my choice of communication! Some of you might choose to exchange e-mail addresses. Communicating by e-mail is fine as long as you know what the person looks like! NEVER give any personal information about yourself over the internet unless you met them in person before communicating online. I will talk more about the internet later in this chapter!
6) If we both have time, I'll make time to get together so we can continue to get to know each other in person even though we will still talk on the phone most of the time.
7) Last, if they have proven to me that they can be trusted, I *might* give them my physical address. Personally, unless there is a reason they need my address, I usually give my post office address. <u>I never give my physical address to anyone I have not met!</u>

Think about how well and how long you want to know someone before giving out your e-mail, phone number, or physical address.

Make sure you stay alert after someone becomes your friend.

You have the right and responsibility to tell anyone to "stop" or "don't touch me there." Touch can include anything from touching on the shoulder to being intimate. YOU have control over your body, mind, and emotions! You have the right to accept or reject any kind of touching! **Make your choices** *wisely!*

Anybody includes:
- Family members
- Boyfriend/girlfriend
- Strangers
- Spouse/partner
- Teachers
- Drivers
- Employers/job, coach/co-workers
- People at your place of worship
- Friends

If someone touches you after you have told them to stop:
- **Get away from them**
- Report/tell any adult that you trust that someone is touching you in a way you don't want!
- Make a police report (highly suggested, but optional)

If you choose to use the internet for the reason of meeting people face-to-face and being their friend or date, be very, very careful! If I choose to meet anyone face-to-face that I first met online, the following is *my* safety plan.

The internet is one of my limitations. If someone gives you different information *for staying safe online*, listen to them first!

1) *Never send a picture of yourself* when you first start writing online.
2) Write your first name *only*.
3) I'd need to know enough to verify before I'd choose to talk with them on the phone.
4) If at *any time* I feel threatened, I'd STOP ALL CONTACT!
5) If the person I was writing to or talking to writes or says anything inconsistent to what they have written or said in the past about themself, I'd question them about it. *If* it still doesn't make sense, **I'd stop contact**.

6) If I choose to meet them face-to-face, then I'd exchange pictures so we'd know what each other looks like!
7) If you choose to meet them in person, it would be very smart to meet him/her in public places for the first few months (or longer) for safety!
8) For the first couple of times you meet in person, it may be a good idea to have a friend or family member sit somewhere else in that place and watch how this person treats you. If they feel comfortable, then it would be okay to continue meeting with them in public without anyone around for safety.
9) There are dating services online which help protect people who search for love on the internet. They charge money, but this type of service is worth the price of protecting your life, health, safety, and money. These types of businesses do a background check on anyone you ask them to. They will give you all the necessary information about your prospective date. Why? The reason is to protect you!

If you choose to use a dating service to meet people online, *please* use a business that will research people thoroughly. Please check all the businesses that do this type of work.

Next, when making a choice about your date or who to spend the rest of your life with, it is important to know ahead of time the kind of people that you would consider spending the rest of your life with and who would be a good friend, and who you want to avoid.

*Before I go on, it is important to note that I believe that everyone should be treated equally! *No one should be put down because they are different. Everyone is to be treated with respect for who they are.*

However, it's not the law to be friends with everyone. It is good to be picky about who your friends are, but not too picky. It is nice that our friends come from different backgrounds whether they are younger or older, were born in a different country than you, etc. However, there may be some differences in your personal opinion that are not worth your time or energy to understand. When choosing a date or someone to spend the rest of your life with, be extremely picky! After all, that person is the person you plan on spending most of your time with for the rest of your life.

For example, how would you feel spending the rest of your life with someone much younger or much older than you? If extreme age difference bothers you, don't consider someone who is too much younger or older.

Here are two examples from my life. Most of my friends are my parents' age because I have more in common with their values and morals than I do with people my age and younger. So, I feel the most comfortable with older people. I'm willing to be friends with people my age and younger, especially if they approach me first and don't move the friendship too quickly!

Another example I have had is being misunderstood by people whose second language is English. The first problem is I don't understand the other person's accent. The second problem is the people I've met whose second language is English don't understand riddles and word play. I joke with words without thinking, especially when I'm stressed out. Since they don't understand word play, I choose not to be their friend, but I'm polite to them and respect them.

It may be smart to know the other's sexual orientation—heterosexual, homosexual, bisexual, etc. People across the USA have feelings about whether heterosexuality, homosexuality, or bisexuality is right or wrong. Some people think it's a personal choice. There are people who think it's no one's business except for the people making the decision. There are people who believe that everyone has the right to believe their own way! People's reasons for agreeing or disagreeing with same gender marriages could be for medical, religious, political reasons, etc.

My overall opinion is people should only have sex with one person until one of them dies. Why? To protect everyone's health! I believe in preventing sexually transmitted diseases.

If you have a strong opinion for or against same gender marriages, minorities, or any other equal rights, get educated and vote. If you are interested in what the current law is regarding same gender marriages, call, write or e-mail your state capitol! A question you may want to ask is, "How does your state interpret holy union and domestic partners?"

If you want to change someone's opinion, it is smart to give some facts and reasons. Tell people where you got your information. However, allow them to have their own opinions.

I will give you an example of expressing your opinion. I think people should have sex inside a *legally* binding lifetime relationship! My main reason is religious and my second is health.

I personally believe divorce is okay where there's child abuse. If there is no abuse, *everything* should be done to save the relationship.

- If your relationship needs help, ask your support team about mediation, individual and couples/marriage counseling, arbitration, and reconciliation before divorce is considered!
- I personally think children need two parents.

Children and teenagers have a lot of emotional needs and they want things which cost money. Two parents can meet their children's needs and wants much better than one can. Parents also need "me time" for themselves! After working all day, parents are very tired. When there are two parents, one parent can have "me time" while the other is spending time with the kids and making dinner. The next night, while the other parent takes care of the kids and housework, the other parent can have "me time." They both still have to find one-on-one time with each kid, and they need to find family time!

- Medical reasons

I believe in having sex with one person to protect each other from sexually transmitted diseases (STD). There are some STD's that can lead to more serious health problems in the future. You can only get an STD by having sex with someone who has an STD.

Basically, if you care about your health and want to have a family someday, ***save sex*** for a lifetime relationship!

Two more things I'd like to say about lifetime relationships:

- The next chapter is also about relationships.
- *Never* rush into a legally binding commitment. If you do, you might regret it later. If you or your partner can't wait to have sex, it would be worth it to reconsider your relationship.

Some people choose to live together and never get married. Some choose to live together and if it works out, then they will get married. Others choose to live in different homes until they get married.

In your opinion:

- What are the positives and negatives of cohabitating?
- What are the positives and negatives of dating?

These are some of the things to consider positive or negative:

- Religious beliefs
- How well do you know the other person?

For example, how long have you known them? Have you known them long enough to know you'll be safe?

- Do you want or need to prove to your support team that you can live alone before you live with someone?

If they ask you to live alone or with a roommate before getting into a legally binding relationship, I think the two main reasons for them asking this of you is to see what you would do when you are in the house by yourself. And second, do you know how to protect yourself? If you have trouble with one or both of these problems, hopefully your support team or someone else will teach you the necessary skills!

- Financial reasons?
- If it's only for financial reasons, why not get one or more roommates?
- Are you choosing to live with the person?
- Is this a person you want to live with for the rest of your life?
- Whether you are living alone, with a roommate(s), or living together, *are you staying healthy? Is it a healthy place?*
- Is the place where you are living or want to live safe?

Safe has two meanings. The first meaning is regarding how much space there is compared to how many people live there. For safety reasons, if people want to be roommates, they will have to think carefully through all aspects.

The second meaning of safety is regarding how safe the roommate(s) or the person you love may be. Is the person/people you want to live with abusive verbally, emotionally, mentally, socially, physically, sexually, or in any other way? Do a complete and honest assessment of answering these questions!

You always have the option to break off a relationship. Please consider telling the other person why you are breaking up if it is safe to do so. You would want someone to tell you **why if they wanted to** break up with you. If someone ever breaks up with you, would it hurt your heart less if they told you why?

From watching other people break up, I have witnessed that the people who never had sex with their date find it easier to break up and they might be able to stay friends. It has been explained to me that the more physical touch there is in a relationship, the harder it is to break up. In my personal opinion, breaking up should be the very last option when a couple is in a legally binding relationship unless there's abuse or someone's life is in danger! Talk to your support team if there's a problem in your relationship!

The reason for me writing the following story is to show you how to put all the pieces together regarding the above list. There is more to the list and the story in the next one or two chapters. Once you see how all the pieces get put together, it will be easier to set your own boundaries!

As a Christian single woman who has disabilities, I would identify who I would be interested in before I would choose where I feel safe meeting the right people. For example, I would choose a man who is polite! He must treat me with respect! He must share _my_ faith, even if he goes to a different church.

I would probably want him to have one or more disabilities, but different disabilities than I have. The reasons I want us to have different disabilities is so he is strong where I'm weak and I'm strong where he is weak. If we have the same disabilities, we'd be weak in the same area which would make life more complicated.

Even people without disabilities have strengths and weaknesses. An example of a couple without disabilities having strengths and weaknesses is a husband and wife team in my church. He works over 40 hours a week and she is the housewife and mom. He gives money to people when he sees them in need.

She has control over the money because she's responsible for the bills. She also knows how much money the family needs to survive. She also puts money aside in case of an emergency.

Can you imagine if both of them were bad with money? What if both were spenders or givers? Their bills would never get paid. The couple and seven kids would have been living on the street a long time ago!

Now that I have established who I would consider dating, I can look at places where I would consider meeting possible dates. The places I would consider looking are churches and religious organizations of my faith, disability advocacy organizations, and religious and disability political groups. Places I would never make new friends are at bars and casinos. For safety reasons, I would never, never ever look for a date or a friend online. Places that I believe are neutral would be public transportation, college, or place of employment.

In fact, I have a friend I met on the city bus. We were friends for one year before we found out we had been going to the same church, but to different services. We were friends for two years before he could think of dating. He was worth waiting for until *he* was ready. The wait was worth it! Giving him the time and space he needed to feel comfortable with dating made him feel safer.

The last thing about dating is the breaking up process. Either person is allowed to break up with the other. If you know yourself and set your boundaries, you have a better chance of choosing someone that you will never have to break up with! If two people decide to break up, there's a better chance that the two of them can remain friends.

When I see my ex-boyfriends, we talk to each other, but we don't hang out in the same places. We don't go to the same church. Instead of trying to change our opinions on our basic values, we agreed that we made better friends than we did as boyfriend and girlfriend.

A basic belief I have from watching other people is not to have sexual contact outside marriage or outside any other legally binding lifetime commitment, because if there's a breakup, you'll have *more respect* for each other during and after dating. The more sexual and/or physical contact a couple has before marriage or a legally binding lifetime commitment, the *less* respect they usually have for each other, and the *harder* it is emotionally *if* the two of you break up.

I know from experience that setting the boundary of saving sex until I get married has helped me respect myself and the other person. Finally, when I broke up with a boyfriend, I gave them a reason!

Now that I have explained the different kinds of boundaries and the process of choosing boundaries by showing you how I chose my standards and set my boundaries, I will help you choose your own standards and set *your own boundaries*. I will assist you by asking you some questions. After you answer the questions, talk to your support team.

TO THE CHOICE MAKER: Here is a list of questions to help you choose your boundaries!

- Are you interested in dating, living with, or having a lifetime commitment with someone?
- Are you interested in dating, cohabiting, or having a lifetime commitment with a man, a woman or both?
- Which living arrangement are you comfortable with? Living apart until there's a lifetime commitment or living together without a legally binding contract.
- What places do you think are safe, unsafe and neutral to meet new friends?
- How slow or fast do you want to get to know someone?
- Would days, weeks, months, or years be long enough to get to know someone?
- How do you want to get to know them? For example, would it be in the place(s) that you already see each other at, or other public places, or in private?
- How long would you want to know the other person before you give them your phone number?
- How long would you want to know the other person before you give them your e-mail address?
- How long would you want to know him/her before you give him/her your physical address?
- Are you interested in meeting new friends or dates through the internet?
- Do you understand and know your space boundaries?
- Are you able to say "No" firmly?
- When you say no and they ignore you, what would your consequences be?

If you don't know some of the answers, ask your support team what they would do if someone ignores their boundaries.

After you answer all the questions you are able to know the

answers to, it is time to tell your support team. They should be quiet until you finish saying everything you want to say. You should be quiet until they are done talking. If you don't know the answers to some of their questions, tell them you'll find out the answers and get back to them.

TO SUPPORT TEAM: Only ask questions that are important and critical to know. If you don't *need* the answers, don't ask! Be willing to share your answers so they feel safe giving you their answers, especially when they are nervous. If they don't know the kind of answer you are looking for, ask it in a different way or give them an example.

TO BOTH OF YOU: If your support team is concerned for you in any way and can explain their reason(s) for waiting until a later time to date or get into a legally binding lifetime contract, trust their advice. If you don't understand, ask someone else on your support team to explain that person's point of view and then make your choice. Know yourself well enough by setting your standards and boundaries!

Chapter 13

Dating and Marriage: Protecting Yourself from Sexual Harassment

The first guy I was interested in was very good looking in my opinion. All the girls liked him! He was a partier. I wanted to party and I wanted to dance. Someone finally explained to me that the parties I was interested in going to included smoking, alcohol, *illegal* drugs, and premarital sex. I was shocked and disappointed! I assumed, if they were telling me the truth, these teenagers would be arrested for breaking the law because they were too young to smoke and drink. *Illegal drugs were and will never be legal at any age (except marijuana)!*

I never dated him because we were too different, and I am glad because he dropped out of high school after his junior year and became a teenage alcoholic. The Lord provided my parents to protect me from being emotionally hurt by this relationship.

As a sophomore, a gentleman from the school choir, John, invited me to his youth group. Considering that neither of us had a driver's license and I already attended church, John wrote a letter to my parents. Mom said, "Yes." I went and I liked it, so they let me continue going.

Eventually, I started attending that church on Sunday mornings also. This was in October 1987. In March 1988, I accepted Jesus Christ into my heart and became a born-again Christian. This began a new spiritual journey for me. *This is when I made a choice about God in my life!* I no longer went to church because I had to. I wanted to!

My parents gave me the freedom to choose between going to John's church or their church. They allowed _me_ to be different from them! As a senior, John wanted me to start a Bible Club in the high school. I laughed and said, "Yeah, right, whatever you say." After that I didn't think much about it.

I share details about my faith because faith helped me make

my own choices! (It still helps me.)

I am continuously getting questions and comments like, "How did you get your parents off your back?" "I want to get married." Therefore, I am sharing how my faith in God helped me do everything all U.S. citizens should have the right to do!

The summer after I trusted the Lord, I was at a friend's house. I was 17 years old. His dad had this very strange game of guessing people's weight that made me feel extremely uncomfortable. Since I didn't know why it felt wrong, I played the game, but I tried to put him in as much pain as possible because it felt wrong! I found out later how bad the game was.

Throughout the day, he had been drinking alcohol but he never offered any to me. He told my parents that he would drive me home and my parents said, "NO!" Their reason for saying no was that they could tell he had too much to drink and should not drive!

It's been more than 20 years and I have seen him twice since then. The first time was by accident and I was safe because there were other people there. The second time I sought him out by phone. He is my friend's guardian and I wanted his permission to do something with his son. I never did get his permission.

Since I am respected by people with disabilities for getting as free from my parents as I want to be and becoming as independent as I wanted to be, including my dating life with some guidelines, I respect the people I have chosen to watch out for me. Therefore, I will continue to be protected on my terms. I have a true example below that explains what I just said.

After I chose my boundaries, I chose my own friends. I chose a group of friends and family members to help me choose if my friends were good, bad or neutral, considering my values. *Get to know people slowly and use caution.*

When I was a junior, there was a guy who had the same physical disabilities as I had, but his disabilities were more severe. However, he tried to undress me in the basement of the school. I prayed that the Lord would protect me and He did; I was able to get away. I ran up the stairs and to the special education room and told the teacher. Her response was, "That's not my problem. You need to learn to get along with your peers."

He stared at me the rest of the school year. I also told my parents and they acted like it was not a big deal. I begged my parents to let me go to a Christian school.

I decided I wanted to be a music pastor's wife and a stay-at-home mom. I came to that decision because of my church values and I committed my life to the Lord. The same year, there was a guy at church that I had a crush on, but I was too shy to tell him. We were friends, but we never dated.

He played many instruments, sang beautifully, and planned on going into the music ministry when he graduated high school. He was an encourager. There were many times I told him I wanted to do something such as be a lawyer, and he told me to go for it in the same encouraging way I encourage anyone who talks to me about being more independent. I'll say to go for it and I would give some suggestions of how to reach their goal!

When I became a senior, my parents forced me to go to the *same* high school instead of letting me go to a Christian school. The guy who tried to undress me in the basement of the school *kept* bothering me in my senior year. My parents said I couldn't go to the Christian school for the following reasons. The first was transportation and I didn't drive. The second was I would graduate a year later which would cost more money. Last, I needed the resource room for some subjects (at the time the Christian school didn't have a resource room)!

Also, as a senior, I met Mark N., who had many talents. He had the ability to be a cook, a weatherman, and an organist. He loved the Lord with all his heart. I was scared to death of the other guy who had tried to undress me, so I stayed very close to Mark. We made a cute couple. Mark and I walked with the opposite limp, so we were constantly walking into each other or away from each other. We were in resource science and choir together the first semester. One day, we were standing in the front of the class and Mark announced, "You are looking at my future bride." He never asked me if I wanted to marry him. I stood there, silently shocked and nodded yes.

He lived in a foster home and his foster dad thought I was a bad influence on him, so we could no longer see each other, and the foster father told another foster child to report back if he saw us talking to each other. I was very upset, but instead of turning to alcohol, drugs, cigarettes, gambling, or another relationship, I was bound and determined to hold onto our relationship until he was allowed to speak for himself.

Remember John's request for me to start a Bible Club? I spent my extra time and energy trying to get a Bible Club in the school. I got 40-45 students to sign a petition for a Bible Club. It would not have taken effect until the year after I graduated, but it would help future students have a positive way of coping with life. While Mark N. was a senior, I became very busy. I made a friend named Mark R. who was a preacher's kid. When Mark N. graduated from high school, he forgot to invite me to his graduation. With pressure from the government, he moved into a group home, so I broke off the engagement.

On the rebound, I got engaged to Mark R. My engagement with Mark R. was shorter than my first one. After I broke up with Mark R., I stopped dating for about two years. Being single was fine with me.

During this time, I became friends with a man who didn't drink, didn't smoke, and didn't use *illegal* drugs; however, he had an anger disorder that was diagnosed as a mental illness. I thought this was safer than anger caused by alcohol or *illegal* drugs. I was wrong!

About nine months after knowing him, he started trying to control my life by demanding my time. I would not give him my time every time he demanded it! He bothered me on the phone and I eventually changed my phone number. He called the phone company and told them that he was my husband and needed my phone number. The phone company called me and told me what happened. I told them not to give him any information about me under any circumstances! I had to vote under my old address for my safety. I also got a post office box. This was a two-year nightmare.

Finally, I had to move because he violated my no contact order. The Sheriff's department refused to help me because I never lived with him, had no children with him, and I was not in immediate danger! The mental health agency would not help. They said he had no control over what he did because of his mental illness.

While waiting to catch a bus, there was a different man who said he used to go to my church. I had seen him on the bus many times in the past. From watching his actions and listening to him talk, I didn't think he ever went to church.

One day, we were waiting for the bus together and he asked me, "Is it all right if I feel you?"

I shouted, "No," and moved to the other side of the bus stop! He respected me. I chose to never speak to him again, but after seven years I'd smile or say, "Hi," in passing, but I still won't talk to him longer than one minute.

In 1995, I went to the Spokane Gospel Jamboree. This was a place where people gathered to sing together two nights a week. It's safer than going to the bar. While there, I met Ron. Ron was interested in me and also had disabilities, just like all the other men I dated in the past. He was a Christian, so I decided to give him a chance. I dated him for two weeks and found out he lied to me twice, so I broke up with him because I'm honest. I hate lying. I can handle different opinions, especially when there's a reasonable conversation! Lying crosses one of my boundaries!

At the Spokane Gospel Jamboree, there was also a young man, Carroll, who ran the soundboard for the musicians. He was 19 years old and in the Air Force stationed at Fairchild, west of Spokane. His eyes were as soft and gentle as the man who wanted to be a music pastor. This was a strange relationship because I was judgmental of people in the military and because I thought war was wrong! I also hated guns. I hated war so much that I participated in a no war protest and stood against going to war.

Dating Carroll was very challenging. He surprised me

because I thought that all people who were in the military who carry guns were loud and controlling. Not Carroll—he was quiet, gentle and peaceful. I was always afraid he would be forced to move to another base or worse yet, be called out to war. We dated for nine months, broke up for nine months, and got back together for two weeks. Then he got out of the military for medical reasons and I never saw or heard from him again.

Part of the reason I never heard from Carroll again was I changed my phone number and moved. Then something *strange* started happening. I started receiving phone calls from Air Force Bases all over the country, but I wasn't afraid. I just thought Carroll was playing cruel jokes on me. But, how could he? I had a new phone number. My phone number had never been in the phone book. After all, no one from the Army, Navy, Marines, or Coast Guard called me; only people from the Air Force Bases and pilots. So why did they start calling me just after my military boyfriend walked out of my life? It was weird. My heart hurt every time I received that kind of call.

Someone finally explained it to me. I knew Carroll well enough to know that he would not give out my number without permission, and I also knew he did not have that much power. I also got four calls from other countries. I also had pilots calling me. They would call me asking for catalogs and wanted to buy different things.

One day, a pilot from California called and said, "I think I got the wrong number."

I said all cheery, "Oh let me guess, you're looking for Survival Inc. The correct number is _____."

He asked me if I got a lot of calls like this and I told him I did. I was so excited that I finally got to ask someone where my number was listed at! He explained that people were finding my phone number in a newly printed survival training handbook.

I said, "That's nice to know. May I have the correct phone number to give to all the other people looking for Survival Inc.?"

He gave me the number and I put the correct number on my answering machine. I played the part of a telephone operator until I changed my number.

We talked for 3½ hours. We talked about flying, religion, the disabled population and what people with disabilities can do, and politics because it was an election year. When we got done talking, he asked, "Do you mind if I call you again?" I told him he could. We became best friends for 22 years.

He's a great friend, but I would never marry or live with him! He came up to visit me and took me flying at a local airport. I got to be the co-pilot, and I absolutely fell in love with flying. I made a choice to never marry a man who was afraid of flying. My parents and Randy also helped me fly to California for my birthday and I got to fly again at his local airport.

Later that year, I met Eli. When we met, he was grief-stricken because two family members died and a third almost died, so I was just his friend. I sat down in front of this person in a wheelchair that was with Eli and in a happy voice asked, "What is your name?"

Eli said, "He can't talk."

I looked at Eli and asked what his name was. He said, "Joshua."

"It's nice to meet you. I am Tiffani."

I was pointing above Joshua's wheelchair and asked Eli, "What's that thing?" It was a kangaroo feeding tower. I asked, "Can he hear?"

Eli said, "Yes."

Finally, I asked, "Can I talk to him?"

Surprised and delighted by my question, Eli said, "Sure!"

I talk to Joshua for 20 minutes before I said another word to Eli. We talked until we got off the bus together and walked 2-3 blocks before we went our separate ways. Later we found out we lived across the street from each other. I saw them on the bus a few more times and always sat beside them. I said, "Hi" to both of them by name and Eli would say, "Who are you?"

I would tell him, "I am Tiffani."

About the fifth time of this, I thought this is crazy. I'm going to find out why Eli never remembers my name when I'm so friendly to them. So, I asked him and he said, "Because I'm legally blind and I can't recognize people by sight. They need to tell me who they are."

On another day, I finally asked Eli, "Don't you ever get a day off?"

Slightly confused, he said, "I'm not his caregiver. I'm his father."

We eventually started spending our free time together. I found out he loved to fly. In fact, he was studying to become an astronaut before he lost his sight.

We shared the same faith. We went to the same church. I found out he used to be a music pastor and I have ministered through music in the choir. We both have disabilities and we both have compassion for people with disabilities. He is a caregiver, and I wanted to be an advocate for people with intellectual disabilities by standing up for their rights and fighting for them to have the same freedoms people without disabilities have! We both love music. He is a semi-professional musician, vocalist and guitarist, and I love to sing.

We also dislike the same things which is very important to us. Neither one of us wants to live with or kiss a smoker! We talk to our family outside when they are smoking. He will wait for his friends to finish smoking and come back inside! We both refuse to drink alcohol! We never hang out with people who drink alcohol to get drunk! (We both have friends who are recovering alcoholics.)

After we knew each other for two years, we decided to start dating. We dated for one year and we felt that God was leading us to marry each other! We were engaged for a long time—at least one year before we married. We knew each other for a total of four years before we got married. *Because of all the things I looked for in a man, I was able to narrow down my choices regarding who I would choose to date to keep myself healthy and safe, and hopefully marry.

Eli passed both my parents' approval and my inspection. He passed my inspection because we have so much in common. The

three best things about Eli are his:
- Faith in God
- Honesty
- Open communication

His faith in God shows through his honesty and open communication! We have the same belief in God, and he also believes that honesty and open communication are the best policies! The more things you have in common with someone, the better the chances are that your relationship will work out. It also takes honesty, open communication, and finding the middle ground. How you handle differences of opinion with others will help you communicate with everyone.

Eli said, "It's traditional for the bride's parents to pay for their daughter's wedding." The reason I share this is, weddings are usually expensive and parents are generally concerned for their children, even when their children are adults. Parents are even concerned for adult children who don't have disabilities. If her parents approve of her fiancé and it is her first wedding, they will probably pay for as much of the wedding that they can afford! (If her parents can only afford to pay for part of the wedding, the bride should pay for the rest of the wedding!) It would be nice to get the approval of the groom's parents too. A honeymoon follows a wedding! The groom usually pays for the honeymoon which is very expensive! It's not tradition, but it is possible that if the groom's parents approve of the bride, they might help the groom pay for the honeymoon.

Domestic partner is a new enough concept that there are no traditions that I'm aware of. If you are interested in being a domestic partner, talk to someone with more knowledge.

Since Eli and I were both adults with two functioning households, when we got married, we were given a lot of cash as wedding gifts. We used the cash to pay for our honeymoon.

If your parents find more bad things than good things in most people, find a trusted friend who you think will tell you the things you need and want to know to make an informed choice about possible friends and things you are interested in. For example, before I made my choice about alcohol, I asked my dad because I was almost 21. I thought it might be wrong, but I didn't know why. My dad responded, "You take medication and I don't!"

I was offended by his tone of voice, so I asked someone else. His response was, "If it's not good for a child, then why is it good for an adult?"

I took that answer to heart about everything from smoking and dancing to sex before marriage and more. Choosing a lifetime partner is very serious, so it would be very wise to explain to your support team why you would want to spend the rest of your life with that person. Let your support team ask all the questions they want to ask, and then answer them *before* making *your final choice*!

TO THE CHOICE MAKER: To protect yourself from sexual harassment, domestic/intimate partner violence, and/or from being stalked, find out what these words mean. It would be a good idea to talk to your power of attorney or guardian and see if they have any concerns.

Sexual harassment, domestic/intimate partner violence, and stalking <u>*are illegal*</u>!

Tell your support team:

- What your boundaries are.
- How you will make others respect your boundaries!

For example, a lot of religious people may say they refuse to have sex before they are married. They may enforce it by going out with their date in public or going on a double date.

Ask yourself about both of your personalities:

- Are you soft spoken? Are they?
- Do you like to fight? Do they?
- Do you like to share in making choices? Do they?
- Do you like to talk through problems? Do they?
- Do you like to be calm? Do they?

For example, I make the choices about things inside the house. Eli makes the choices about the outside of the house. There are two things we consider when making choices about the inside or outside. Can we afford it? Can I, as a person with a physical disability, also use it?

TO SUPPORT TEAM: Accept that your person will have different opinions than you. They will want to date different people that you might not find to be acceptable. If you stop the dating process, they will never be able to know who they would and would not like to date. They won't know why they feel/think the way they do.

I'll never know why I dated a man in the military when I am terrified of guns. However, Carroll had a soft voice, and I assumed all people in the military were mean and loud. Only in my worst nightmare would I have ever considered dating someone in the military or the police. As of my wedding date, I will never date again because I am married.

These are the things protected people should do when learning how to keep themselves safe: They should explain their reasoning *when learning to* make healthy and safe choices! It would be smart to always explain how and why you choose the friends you've chosen!

The motive for wanting to know the choice maker's decisions and reasons is to find out which decisions have been made by them and which decisions they were talked into.

The support team should only have the choice maker explain themselves when they <u>*believe it is necessary*</u> so they don't feel like they're in a courtroom.

If you want them to share their opinion and they don't want to, share your opinion about the same subject and how you made your decision(s) on the same subject!

Chapter 14

Children

As a teenager, I wanted to be a stay-at-home wife and mom when I became an adult. I wanted to run the kids all over town, do the housework and be very active in the community. In my late 20's, I thought having children was a bad idea *for me*!

When I went to school to get a job working with children ages birth through six years, one of my teachers was very discouraging! They knew I had disabilities and thought the accommodations I asked for were unreasonable!

My school counselor told me parenting *my* children would *be different* than taking care of children *professionally*. The reason I was having trouble was I had no fine motor skills in my left hand so changing diapers was difficult for me.

With my learning disability, I struggled with change. I liked things to say the same!

People who have mental health issues and intellectual disabilities have told me horrible true stories about Child Protective Services (CPS) getting involved in their lives *before* or when their child was born. I finally saw it for myself and I was told about this process in one of my classes.

It would be smart if social service agencies would start teaching parents how to be healthy and safe parents when the mother becomes pregnant.

A responsible person would ask for counseling or parenting classes *before* the mother gets pregnant or delivers. From what I have seen, CPS takes children away from parents who have disabilities. They rarely give their children back even when the parents can show that they have learned the skills to be healthy and safe!

When I got married, I acquired children, mostly adults. They were all my husband's children. This makes me a stepmom. One adult son was still living at home and being taken care of because of his intellectual disability. My husband also adopted his grandson. When we got married, we continued to raise the two and the other three had moved out.

At first, my husband was a stay-at-home parent while I was going to school or visiting my friends with intellectual disabilities. Joshua, our adult son, went to be with Jesus. Eli was without a job for five months. I have no natural children. All the children I write about are my husband's children.

In the next few paragraphs, I am going to give my personal observations from watching people and the things I personally learned in a class titled, "Understanding Child Abuse." I am going to talk about the different kinds of parenting.

One popular kind of parenting that society tends to look down on is single parenting. The reason society seems to look down on single parenting is, they usually don't have enough money to raise kids! I have watched single parent and two-parent families and have noticed single parents have less patience because they are more exhausted than two-parent families! The reason for this is, when one parent is doing *all* the housework and earning *all* the money for the household, they are more tired than two people who are sharing the childcare, working outside the home, and doing housework, etc. I know women who have felt cheated because they got pregnant when they were teenagers.

Another reason society might look down on single parent families is when a married couple needs a little government help, a lot of times the government can't or won't help the two-parent family or tells them they are eligible for something they already have and don't need. I have witnessed a married couple, who had four children, apply for medical assistance and were denied but were told they were eligible for food stamps. Their rent, electricity and phone bills had been paid and they had enough food in the house. However, the state said they were eligible for food stamps. Single parent families are often eligible for everything they apply for. Sometimes, they are totally dependent on the government and that angers the taxpayers.

Married couple parenting is a kind of two-parent family that is very common. Money-wise, it is the best kind of family, because some jobs will give the spouse and the children medical benefits. Churchgoers view being married first and having children second as "the right way." From people I talked to who had children outside marriage, most of them said if they could do it again, they would get married before having children. Most of the people I talked to were churchgoers. Some said they would have had fewer children. Other people thought they would save more money or start buying a house before having kids, and others would choose to never have kids.

Blended families are when both spouses bring their own children into another marriage. The newest parent to the child and the newest child to the adult is the step side of the family meaning the stepparent/stepchild. The parent that is originally attached to the child is the natural parent.

When my husband and I got married, he brought four children and I brought no children into our marriage.

Blended families are probably the most common two-parent families because the divorce rate is so high! Since this group of two-parent families are also married, they get the same medical benefits that first-time married couples get.

Due to the special problems blended families have, some churches have a ministry geared for blended families. They may have ministries geared for different ages of children—elementary, middle school and high school kids who are stepchildren. There might also be a ministry for stepparents.

There are church people who will judge others no matter what. If someone's opinion is that important to you, then you should make them explain their point of view! I will never let a judgmental person bother me whether they are a family member, someone who works in a social service agency, or a friend. If it's important to me, then I make them explain why they are judging me. My faith in Jesus Christ is my primary way of keeping my self-respect along with ignoring the comments of judgmental people.

The natural parent is the parent that is responsible for the child before they get married again. Parents must do everything they can do to keep their children safe and protected from dangerous adults.

In my personal opinion, living together sets a bad example for children commitment-wise. Why? When adults walk away from a commitment anytime there is a disagreement instead of working things out, the children learn to avoid confrontation. Instead, the parents should learn how to properly confront a problem and work out their differences!

Here is an example of proper confrontation: Let's say a cashier at the store took more money than they should have for something you bought. When you notice this, it is proper to go back to the cashier **_with the receipt_** and get the correct amount of money back. It would be wrong to say, "Oh well," and walk away!! *No one has the right to take money that doesn't belong to the business!*

The worst part about living together, in my opinion, is most people who live together do so to pay the bills, and not love. Even if that's your reason and you are not looking for a relationship, anyone you live with still needs to be a safe person!

If you are going to live together or have a roommate(s), you *need to choose carefully* if you want to have child(ren). You need to make healthy and safe choices if you want to keep your kids. Relatives and your support team need to know that your children are safe with any adult that you live with or that's around your child(ren).

Your living arrangement is a choice, but be careful when a child is in your home because Child Protective Services has the right to come in and take your child(ren) away if they think the children are in any kind of danger!!

Foster parents are parents who take children into their home who need a _temporary_ place to stay! Foster children might live in many foster homes before they are adopted.

Foster children could have any of the following problems. They may have been:

- Neglected
- Abandoned
- Abused

There are many types of abuse:
- Emotional
- Mental
- Verbal
- Physical
- Sexual
- Spiritual

Children might be in the foster care system for other reasons. Possible reasons:
- Their parents died.
- Their parents broke the law.
- Their parents couldn't afford to take care of them.
- The State won't allow parents who have disabilities to raise their children *unless they prove they can.*
- The parents can't deal with the child's disabilities.

There may be other reasons I can't think of.

Children may come into the foster care program with the following:
- Behavioral problems
- Mental health issues
- Parents or children with drug and/or alcohol problems
- Parents or children who have intellectual and/or physical disabilities
- Parents or children are in trouble with the law

Talk to your support team if you want information on the foster care program in your state!

Every state has their own foster care laws. Some states may pay a person to be a foster parent. How much? I don't know. It might depend on how hard a child is to take care of, how much damage a child does to property, and/or the age of the child. Call or e-mail the social service agency that runs the foster care program in your state. You can look up the foster care laws for your state if you are interested.

Foster parents *must be* emotionally strong to handle the state bringing a child in and pulling a child out, sometimes without any warning and with no time to say goodbye. That's difficult!

I am aware of one case where a foster parent called the state and told them to get the child out of their home because the foster child kicked and bruised another child. The child that was kicked was 100% unable to protect himself. This foster child was very unsafe! All children must be safe at all times! You must protect your natural children and foster children *equally*! If it's impossible to keep your natural children safe, stop being a foster parent until it's *safe for everyone*! Let the state place the foster children in a different environment.

Some foster children might damage property or break the law in other ways. What would you do if or when foster children does something wrong? Be careful and creative! From things I learned in an *Understanding Child Abuse* class, I will never be a foster parent. I don't have enough energy and I don't have the emotional strength to cope with the state popping in and taking a child or dropping a child off <u>*unannounced*</u>, especially in the middle of the night.

Adoption is legally giving child(ren) a new set of parents. The legal process of adoption is different in every state! The legal process is different in every country of the world. There are family adoptions where grandparents have adopted their grandchildren. Other family members can apply to be adoptive parents only when the state says that both natural parents are <u>not</u> able to raise their kids.

Strangers can also adopt children! However, whether it is a family or stranger adoption, the state must be the one to choose the adoptive parents!

If you are interested in adopting a child or teenager from

another country, there is a whole different process. The government must be involved in the adoption process for the protection of everyone involved.

If you are interested in adopting a child, contact your state social services agency.

My experience of family adoption is the birth parent making our life a nightmare. My husband adopted his grandson. Life was hard on him because there were times the grandson or I asked him to do something that he legally would not do. Most of the time it was the birth mother who wanted something. He had to make the hard decisions for his grandson's health and safety. His mom was angry that I could legally make choices for her child.

TO THE CHOICE MAKER: Before I go any further, I want to make something clear about a two-parent family. Even though I write about two-parent families in a very positive way, if there is _ever_ any danger to any child(ren), talk to your support team to make plans together for _everyone's_ safety and health!

There's no time to make a plan in an emergency! Your support team might have to choose what to do for _your children_!

When the danger is over, there will be time to talk it out. Find out what the future plans are for keeping children and people who have disabilities safe. (Children's safety must come _before_ the adult's safety.)

- If a parent has a temporary medical crisis, where does the parent(s) want their children placed until the crisis is over?
- Where would the parent(s) want their children placed if the emergency is permanent?

In case there are other kinds of temporary emergencies, the types of things you would want in a plan are:

- Who should the babysitter call if the parents are late and are not answering their phone?
- How long should the babysitter wait before they should be concerned? (Just in case there is a traffic jam. Should

the babysitter wait an extra half hour before they start to be concerned?)
- Is there anything the children will need (i.e., medication) if you are running late?
- How can the babysitter calm the children down if you are running late?

There should also be things in place to protect you:
- A medical alert necklace or bracelet
- Have a medical advance directive
- Have a mental health advance directive (if needed)!

If your relationship is unsafe and you have children, there's counseling for the victim. There is also counseling available for the accuser if they will accept the help! There are different ways to get away and to stay away from someone for a short time or forever. The person who is being hurt needs to learn new boundaries and why the new boundaries are needed while the support team stays temporarily in control! The support team _needs_ to stay in control _until_ your new boundaries have been set and kept!

However, if you want to go out with someone, but it's a bad time, tell them and maybe suggest another time. You might tell them *when is* a good time to get together.

There are ways that the law recognizes that two people are staying away from each other, so the court does not have to be a part of. It is still legal and within the law. However, if you avoid going through the court, you are showing that you might want to get back together with him or her in the future.

Separation means getting away from each other for a short amount of time, seeing how things go, and possibly getting back together at a later date. The date needs to be agreed upon by both people in the relationship. Mediation is finding a neutral person who will help everybody come up with a workable plan for them and keep it out of the court system. Arbitration means all people involved have to go a step above mediation and have someone else put an agreement on paper that is legally binding like a contract. There is also marriage and couples counseling. If both people will accept their share of the good things and the bad things, marriage and couples counseling works. It doesn't work if one person is blaming the other person for everything that has gone wrong and is going wrong in their relationship.

*IF an accused person is being accused or convicted of domestic violence, **perpetrator's treatment might be available**!

*Parenting plans, supervised visits, paying child support, etc. are some ways an accused or convicted parent might be able to work his or her way back to being trusted again.

My husband taught me that our children's needs come before the parents' needs. Needs include:

- Housing
- Electricity
- Clothing
- Food
- Quality time every day with every child
- Childcare
- Have a plan when a child gets sick at school
- Phone

It is necessary to have a phone so the doctors, your child's school, etc. can be called in case of emergency! Parents' needs come second! Childcare is necessary until children are old enough to be alone. Making plans for a sick child doesn't need to happen until the child starts school.

When it comes to everyone's wants, if there is enough money in the budget, it would be nice to consider every family member's wants; but there's no rule that says anyone's wants comes before someone else's. When there's not enough money for everyone to have what they want, every family has its own way of choosing if and when the wants get met.

When a child enters school, music and/or sports may become important to your child. Extra activities cost more. Some families might be eligible for scholarships. However, music and sports are wants, not needs! If there are grants or other ways to pay for any music and/or the sports your children are interested in at school, look into grant money to see if your family is eligible.

Our child went to a private school and the parents had to pay for afterschool sports. Since sports are a want, he had to keep his grades up and be more responsible in other areas. As long as he kept his grades up, we agreed to do our part to keep him involved in sports. That included asking for help when he needed it. Those rules applied to music too!

Before you make a choice to be a parent, it would be a wise idea to read up or have a friend help you look up information on every kind of parenting you are interested in becoming. Also, it would be wise to talk to the kind of parents you are interested in becoming, like natural, blended, etc. This kind of research helps everybody make choices. You can gather information from the news, library, relatives, radio, and your support team.

Ask your family members or friends what they see as your strengths and weaknesses. (I would choose friends and family from different walks of life, like someone from church, friends who have the same disabilities as myself, my best friend, and my mom.)

From what I have seen, the people who only get practical advice get very discouraged! The people who only talk to people who are spiritual people are given so much positive information that they are not prepared to be a parent. Spiritual people know how to say what is positive and good, such as they're honest, etc. However, what does honesty have to do with the ability to change diapers or financially support a child?

The people who are giving spiritual and practical information are wonderful. Sometimes, spiritual people or people without religion can give you both spiritual and practical information.

I have spiritual friends who helped me raise my children with the values I wanted them to have. They encouraged me. I have one practical friend who helped me with things I needed to know to keep my children safe!

Your practical friends can help you by taking an honest look at <u>your ability</u> to take care of children or <u>your ability</u> to learn. If the people you trust have concerns, find out what their concerns are. Then find out how to eliminate those concerns.

You and your support team need to feel free to point out your strengths and weaknesses. It needs to be done in a way society calls constructive criticism. By taking parenting classes, it may help you to know what to expect from a child. The one requirement for the parents: Both parents *must attend all* the parenting classes! These classes can provide needed accommodations to people with disabilities to make their home healthy and safe. The accommodations may be education and knowledge of the agencies in the community that serve and help children and parents.

***Asking to take parenting classes before a baby is born is responsible, <u>whether you're the mom or the dad</u>*!

Ask yourself the questions below before you talk to your support team. Here is a list of questions to find out your strengths and weaknesses:

- Is it easy for you to get to places on time?
- Is it easy for you to get ready to leave?
- Is it easy for you to remember to make your child's and your doctor appointments?
- Is it easy for you to remember to cancel doctor appointments if there is a reason you cannot show up?
- Do you believe there are times when you are allowed to cancel a doctor's appointment?
- If so, when is it okay?
- If not, why not?
- In what amount of time do you have to cancel an appointment? (Every doctor's office has different rules regarding canceling and rescheduling.)

The reason these questions are so important is that when it

comes to a child and their medical appointments, the professionals working for and around you need and want to make sure you can and will do everything your children needs.

By showing them that you know the right thing to do, your doctor, counselor, other healthcare professionals, etc. will be your best advocates!

If you are considering finding a partner who would be a good parent to your children, consider asking yourself the following questions:

- Do they have a job? (Do you have a job?)
- How much money do they make a month? (How much money do you make a month?)
- How much money do they save a month? (How much money do you save a month?)
- How much money do they spend every month on their required bills? (How much money do you spend every month on required bills?)
- How much money do they spend on having fun every month? (How much money do you spend on having fun every month?)
- Do they want children? (Do you want children?)
- Are they willing to sacrifice financially for children? (Are you willing to sacrifice financially for children?)

You two would need to talk over how you will pay for the children if and when they come into the picture. These are possible suggestions:

- If only one person is working, can the second person get a job?
- Cut your spending.

You can do this by cutting some of your bills (i.e., getting a cheaper cable or dish plan, cheaper cell phone plan, or spend less for other things) or get a better paying job.

- *If both of you* already have one job, are either of you willing to get a second job?

Look at yourself physically, emotionally, and your thinking ability for short and long range.

- What are your strengths and abilities?
- What are your weaknesses that are not your disabilities?
- What are your weaknesses that are because of your disabilities?

The weaknesses that are not disabilities will be easier to correct. The weaknesses that are caused by disabilities are going to be very difficult to make stronger, but this is where making accommodations or compromising works best! An example of a compromise: People who are deaf, learning to read lips. An example of accommodations: People who are deaf having a sign language interpreter and equipment that would help, such as a flashing light for when the doorbell or phone rings.

Physically:

- Can you walk?
- Can you use your arms?
- Can you use your wrists?
- Can you use your fingers and fine motor skills?

If you have any problems with any of the above things, how do you accommodate them?

If you are really strong, you need to be careful so that you won't hurt a child accidently! Adults have more strength than newborn babies! Adults are taller and heavier.

Emotionally:

- Do you get easily stressed out?
- If so, how often?
- What do you do to calm yourself down?
- Do you have anxiety attacks?

- How do you reduce your stress and anxiety?
- Do you hear voices?
- If so, how do you recognize the real world from the voices?
- Do you have mood swings? How severe?
- If so, how do you handle them?
- How do you deal with negative feelings such as being depressed, etc.?
- How do you handle your anger?
- How do you deal with other's anger?
- When you are having emotional problems, how will you keep your children safe?

Mental or thinking ability:
- How often do you remember important things that people tell you?
- How easy is it for you to take notes?
- Do you remember to write appointments on your calendar?
- How do you look up addresses and phone numbers?
- Are you a quick thinker?

For example, if the phone rings at the same time someone knocks on the door and you are cooking, in what order would you take care of everything?

- Can you tell the difference between medical problems that can be handled at home, problems that require minor emergency, or those that need to be handled at the hospital?
- If not, do you have friends or family members you can call and ask when something is medically wrong?
- Do you know how to keep from burning yourself?
- IF you burn yourself, what would you do?

Burn accidents *can happen to anyone*! How you handle ***any*** *accident* is very important.

- Do you know how to prevent accidents?
- Are you a self-starter or do you need someone to talk you through every step?

TO THE BOTH OF YOU: If you still want to be a parent, I would strongly recommend strengthening one weakness at a time!

- Talk to someone on your support team regarding money issues about children.
- Talk to your support team about all the things including plans of how to strengthen your weaknesses or work with them or around them.

You and your support team can each pick out one or two weaknesses to work on. After your support team has listened to you, it would be very smart to let them tell you which one they think would be best for you to work on at this time so you can be a better parent and let them know which one you want to work on. Talk it over and the two of you can choose which one you are going to work on. If your support team thinks you can strengthen two weaknesses at the same time, then work on two of them!

*When you are ready to have a child or children it is time to go see all of your doctors.

**Remember life can quickly change. It's always smart to have one or more backup plans in case of an emergency. *Emergencies just happen! They are never planned!*

Finally, it's okay to wait to have children! Some people wait until:

- They are married.
- They are financially stable.
- They have finished college.

In fact, some people choose to finish college before they get married. I have gone to college while I was single, while I was engaged, and while I was married *with* children. From experience, I can tell you it is much easier to concentrate on school without children around.

Think carefully before you choose to have children. Having children is a lifetime commitment. Once you are pregnant or you have adopted a child, there is no backing out, even if your health goes bad or you have money problems in the future!

Chapter 15

Long Distance Traveling

I can't be specific about some places I have traveled to. As you read the parts where people have traveled consider:

- Did the person make plans before they traveled?
- Did they choose to travel with little or no planning?
- Did someone in the house have vacation time?
- Did someone in the house have to take time off work?
- Is anyone going on the trip with you? If so, does everyone going on the trip plan to share the cost? If so, what is each person paying for?

The more people that share in the cost, the cheaper it is, so everyone will have more spending money. In 1993, I went to Sacramento with a man I was not married to. We went for religious reasons. We both saved enough money for our own "round-trip" bus ticket.

We had saved money to eat at restaurants. We cut costs by sometimes going to a sit-down restaurant, buying one plate of food, sharing the cost and the food. This was our primary way of sharing expenses. Due to my religious and personal boundaries I refused to share a motel room with him. I brought enough money to pay for my own room. This man was very angry with my boundary. He didn't bring enough money. He argued with me in front of other people, trying to get me to change my mind; however, I stood my ground!

- It would have been smart to have taken a little extra money in case there was an emergency.

Possible emergencies could be:

- Our bus could have broken down.
- There could have been a family emergency.

- Taxi fare in case the bus stopped running or if there was no bus available.
- Hotel or motel money for an extra night if you can't get home in time.

I was too young to realize anything could have gone wrong. At age 22, I expected perfect weather in Sacramento since I grew up in the snow and ice and always heard about sunny California.

In the future, I would probably never leave town with a man that I'm not married to unless my parents approved of the man. However, I chose to travel with this man and God protected me! I was already very cautious because he was already trying to get me to do things I didn't want to do at home! Because he was trying to get me to do things I didn't want to, *I should never have left with him*!

In 1994, I went to Olympia, the capitol in Washington State. This is the city where legislators, senators and the governor meet to make, modify, or repeal laws. I wanted to talk to my state senator and representatives.

A group of people with disabilities went with an agency to advocate for people with many different kinds of disabilities. They took as many people with disabilities from the community as they could, along with as many employees as they had to for their health and safety. Caregivers, family members and anyone else interested in helping advocate for people with disabilities were welcome to come. Everyone could advocate for themselves by telling as many politicians as possible about a part of their life and how social service agencies help them in their daily life. There were many agencies that serve the disabled population who went to Olympia that day.

It was called Advocacy Day and it was only for one day, so there were no motel costs. The agency I went with paid for everyone's airplane ticket, but everybody had to pay for their own food.

I still didn't know the importance of having extra money in case of an emergency. Since I was with a group and under the watchful eyes of the agency, I felt safe that the agency would have gotten me out of trouble if there was trouble.

Later in 1994, I went back to Sacramento on the Greyhound bus. I went for the same religious reason as I did in 1993. My mom and I made plans for me to meet a woman in Pasco, Washington who was also going to Sacramento. I rode alone on the bus until I got to Pasco, and then she joined me. When she got on the bus, we rode together and we got a motel room together for our safety. We split the cost of the motel room.

In 1995, two of my friends and I got on a Greyhound bus and went to Tacoma, Washington for the same religious reason that I had gone to Sacramento twice before. My bus ticket to Tacoma was cheaper because Tacoma was closer than California.

I saved enough money to pay for my own room because both of my friends smoked. One friend chose to smoke in the room, and my other friend chose to smoke outside. (Smoking inside was legal back then.)

Remember earlier when I talked about setting your own boundaries regarding what is acceptable? My boundary was nobody was going to smoke in my motel room. I chose to share a motel room with the outside smoker. The other friend got her own room.

Since all three of us were on a strict budget, we looked for a motel that was reasonably priced, in a safe area, and close to the arena. We searched until we all agreed on the motel. We stayed together the whole time!

I took my next trip in 1998, and I was still single. (I will talk about my friend's trip later in this chapter.) The main thing to know is he came up and met my parents before I went down there. All seven days was a birthday present from my parents and friend. My parents bought my round-trip ticket. My friend, Randy, paid for my stay in a motel room because we wanted to be under a different roof at night; he wanted his privacy and I had only seen him face-to face one time. The other reason was my religious beliefs.

When I got off the airplane, he was there to greet me and got me checked into my motel room. We also drove around the Pacific Coast Highway. While driving around on the highway, I got to see the Pacific Ocean. Later that day, we went to the Chamber of Commerce. The Chamber of Commerce gives out information to promote the town and its businesses. There is also a section for visitors who want to know about the tourist attractions.

The second day we went to Universal Studios. Universal Studios makes television shows and movies. We watched an animal show and I got teased by Charlie Chaplin. Charlie teased me by tickling me with a straw of hay. He teased everyone he could! He did this to make the crowd laugh. He also dressed up funny. We got taken around by a tour guide. He showed us movies and TV shows that had been made and were currently being made at the time I visited.

I noticed Randy made a lot of U-turns. It looked like California and Washington driving laws were different. So, we went and got a California State driver's guide to compare laws. I also got to meet his family.

Just about everyone in Washington I know wants to go to Disneyland. He took me and I hated it! The lines were too long! We stood for so long my feet hurt and I got too tired! I just wanted to sit down or lay down! I wished I'd had a wheelchair while at Disneyland! We went driving around and to his apartment to rest. I got to see his large model airplane. We went and visited with a Christian family in his apartment complex, and I met his landlord.

Day five, we went to Olivera Street. Olivera Street is a street where people sell Mexican things. This is one time in my life I was glad to have someone with me because I don't know Spanish and was in an unfamiliar place. Later that day, we went and hung out at the motel, looked at all the different shops, and sat in the lobby.

On day six, we went to the Reagan Museum to see all the good and bad things done while Ronald Reagan was an actor, the Governor of California, and the President, along with some of the things that have happened to the Reagan family in their personal lives. I remember the work he had done regarding tearing down the Berlin Wall. The Berlin Wall was torn down one year after he was out of office. Nancy Regan had a program called *Just Say No To Drugs*. They also had things in a museum about Alzheimer's disease. Alzheimer's disease is a disease that he got after he no longer had a political job. At this time, there is no cure for Alzheimer's but there is a handful of medications that can help individuals who have it. They have information about other illnesses and diseases that the President's other family members had over the years. They also had quilts hanging up on the walls in one room of the museum. Later, we went to a small airport and went flying for two hours in a 110 Cessna.

Day seven was my last day in California, so I checked out of the motel and put my things in Randy's car for the day. Then we headed off to Warner Brothers. Warner Brothers makes TV shows and movies, just like Universal Studios does. Warner Brothers made a show that I loved to watch. While at Warner Brothers, I got to see the car that was always jumping over things that were blocking the road such as a creek, cliff or dead end. After we left Warner Brothers, we drove by a place I would have been interested in working at if I had moved to California. During the seven days I was there, my friend took me out to eat and bought all my meals. My favorite place to eat was Sizzler. We went there as many times as possible because there were no Sizzler's open back home. We also went to other restaurants. My friend paid for my meals as part of my birthday present. Finally, he took me to the airport and got me on the plane. Mom was waiting for me at the airport and brought me home.

In 2000, my fiancé's father had a stroke. I got a credit card with a fixed rate. Ask your support team to explain what a fixed rate and a variable rate is. My parents disapproved. Their opinion was if you don't have enough cash, don't buy it!

However, my parents approved of the man I wanted to leave town with and understood that there was a possibility that this might be his last chance to see his father alive. It was important to me to give my fiancé emotional support, so I got a credit card.

Three months earlier, I had an emotional breakdown and he was there for me emotionally, so my parents provided me with a calling card so I could be there for Eli. It was cheaper than using my cell phone (at that time)! The reason my parents provided me with a calling card is so I could keep myself emotionally calm so I could be emotionally stable for Eli.

In 2002, we went to Hawaii for our honeymoon for eight days and seven nights. Since we were older and living alone before we got married, we got a lot of cash gifts for our honeymoon. Both of us were good at saving money, so when we chose to get married, the money we saved in our own accounts and cash gifts were spent on our honeymoon.

We went to an island that had public transportation, so we didn't have to get a cab unless we wanted to! We had money to buy little souvenirs to show that we really went to Hawaii. We sent some people postcards, we bought leis, and we bought a photo album with the seven islands of Hawaii on the front cover. We went to Waikiki Beach and on a dinner cruise around Diamond Head. (If you get seasick or have balancing problems, you would not like this cruise! It will make you sick!) It was fun in our opinion, but because of the waves I had no balance! We also went to a restaurant on the 23rd floor called Top of Waikiki. It spins like the Space Needle in Seattle, WA. We saw an Elvis impersonator who was very down-to-earth. We flew around Hawaii in a little airplane. We got to visit the capitol of Hawaii, Honolulu. A tour guide took us around and he took us to the Governor's office. Anyone on the tour who wanted to sit behind the Governor's desk and pretend to sign a bill, got to. I chose to. My bill was titled *Disability Rights*.

We also went to hear S.O.S. sing. They are a group of seven men dressed up in funny costumes. They change their vocalists every once in a while. We also went to a luau and got pictures of a lighthouse while we were there. Part of the motel cost was getting breakfast every morning. Every morning we went down and got a "free" breakfast. We ate breakfast there every morning except one. That morning we had breakfast delivered to our room.

Our children didn't come with us. Eli's family watched them while we were on our honeymoon. By having our family watch them, we did not have to pay for childcare. When we went to Eli's 35th class reunion, his family handed our boys back to us. While on the 35th class reunion, we stayed in a motel room with two queen-sized beds. Our boys slept in one bed while Eli and I slept in the other bed. (To save money, if you only need one bed, check to see if a one or two bedroom is cheaper!)

Eli also took me on a tour around the town that he used to live in. He showed me places that were special to him. One place I was shown was called "the big house" which was three floors high. Eli did a lot of remodeling to the big house in the late 1980's and early 1990's. We also went to his favorite restaurant.

In reading about the next two vacations, look for the emergencies:

- Did they have to use their emergency fund? An emergency fund is money you *don't plan on* spending on your trip but will spend if you *need to*!
- If there was a crisis and they didn't use their emergency fund, what did they do?

If you can't answer this question, it would be smart to ask for some additional advice from your support team!

Christmas 2003, Eli and I went back to see his parents. We let our grandson, who was the only child we were taking care of at that time, stay with another family member. This was the first time we had taken a trip when Eli was out of work, but maybe the last time we would see his dad alive. His dad was in his early 80's.

To save money and to spend time with Eli's best friend and

college roommate he had met 25-30 years earlier, Eli wanted to stay with his friend. I **did not**! I almost stayed home because I thought it was ***dangerous***. I just had a feeling that Eli's friend had no morals because Eli had told me things he did when they were college roommates over 25 years ago. I was unable to explain why I felt so uncomfortable; I just did.

Eli hadn't seen this man for over 30 years. Everything Eli said about him sounded dangerous because when they were both single and roommates, if a woman wanted to date the roommate, it was accepted and understood by both men that the lady could choose which roommate she wanted. Eli had the opinion that women have a mind of their own and he was never going to force a woman to stay with him if she wanted to go out with his roommate. However, his roommate treated women very differently. He treated women as if they were on earth for a *man's pleasure only* and he didn't think he should have to think about a woman's needs, wants, desires, wishes, or feelings. This is how Eli talked about him and I had no proof that he had changed!

Eli thought his friend would respect his marriage vows. Eli was wrong, surprised, and angry to find out that he had to tell him that there were new boundaries by saying, "My wife is off limits!" I told Eli how this man violated me many times.

We spent the rest of Christmas vacation at Eli's parents' house. When we got home, Eli confronted him by e-mail and broke off their friendship! Eli trusts me more after going through that experience.

We would have had to stay somewhere else even if this guy was nice. The reason: I was having medical problems from his house being way too cold. It was too cold because he turned down the heat and he kept his hot water tank off to save money!

MY FRIEND'S TRIP

My friend from California came to visit me in January 1998. When he headed home, he hit "black ice" 80-90 miles outside of the town I lived in. He crashed his car against a wall of rocks crushing his rear window. No one was sitting in the backseat when the accident happened.

Someone called the state patrol on their cell phone. The state police helped my friend and gave him a ride to the nearest gas station. My friend called my parents to see if they could pick him up and bring him back. My parents were home, had no other plans and they had the money to get gas. My parents picked me up, got gas, and went and got him. We took him to the Spokane airport. He bought an airline ticket. We stayed with him until he got on the plane.

TO THE CHOICE MAKER: Save money for all the things you need by asking yourself these questions when planning for a trip:

1) Where are you going?
2) Why are you going there?
3) How are you going to get there?
4a) Where are you going to sleep?
4b) How many nights do you plan on sleeping in a hotel or motel? The days of the week and the dates are important, especially if you're traveling during a holiday!
5) Where will you eat? Will you be eating at restaurants, at family's or friend's houses, or will your hotel/motel room have a kitchen in it?
6) How are you going to get around town?
7) You will need to have extra money to pay for things you want to buy such as things that are special to that area.
8) Emergency fund – How much money do you think you need to put aside in case of an emergency?
9) How many days will you be at your destination?

Here's another group of questions that will help you plan for a trip. These include making plans to leave and getting emotional support while you are gone:

1) If you have kids in school or when members of family work, you need to plan your vacations around everyone's schedule. Vacation time for children is called spring break, Christmas break, or summer vacation. Children also have three-day weekends throughout the school year due to holidays. Sometimes, people have to take a leave of absence.
2) Do you need to put a hold on the newspaper and the mail while you are gone, or have someone get it for you?
3) Do you need someone to take care of your home, pets, plants, etc. while you are gone? If you need someone to help you, you have three options! Choose one of them so your home, pets and plants will be taken care of while you are gone!
   A) Get a house sitter. A house sitter is someone who lives in your home while you are out of town and will leave when you get home! While they are staying at your home, they will pick up your mail and newspaper every day until you get home. They will also take care of your pets and plants. Your home should look as clean as it was when you left! The benefit of having someone stay in your home while you're gone is to keep the robbers away! *Be sure you choose someone you trust 100% to have a key to your home!* If anything is missing, it would be easy to accuse your friend of stealing when you might have misplaced what you were looking for; meaning you found it later.
   B) Have someone come to your home 1-2 times a day to check on everything. In the morning, they need to get your newspaper and feed your pets (and possibly walk the pets). Later that day, possibly at nighttime, they need to come back to get the mail, water the plants, and see if your pets still have enough food and water. Then they come back in the morning. If your choice is A or B, you'll have to trust the person you

choose to watch your home because they will need a temporary key until you get back into town.

C) The last choice would be to have your pets and plants taken care of at a friend's house until you come home! Put a hold on your mail and newspaper! A 'hold' temporarily stops the mail and newspaper delivery until you ask them to start sending it again. Remember to take the hold off when you come home! Make a list of things you need so you remember everything. **_Keep your medication with you at all times_** so if your luggage gets lost, you can still take your medication! If you are taking a plane, bus, train, or boat, remember your ticket! Put the ticket in your wallet or purse!

Plan how much money you think you will need to cover the cost of the first set of questions related to money.

1) Do you have enough medication to last through your trip without having to go to a pharmacy?
2) Do you need or want any help from family or friends? (Buying over the internet is cheaper but can be more financially dangerous. I will never give my credit card information on the internet.) Another thing, do you need help packing? Packing is difficult for me, so I ask for help.
3) Do you need to have any emotional support from family or friends? (For example, on one trip I took, my parents gave me extra emotional support by giving me a calling card for the trip.)

I would strongly encourage you to talk to your support team about your plans so you don't have any unpleasant surprises. One or two of them should be people who share your values. Some people might choose friends in Alcoholics Anonymous. A second person could be your best friend. Your third and fourth people should be one man and one woman that you trust who have been to the place you want to go.

If you are unable to find anyone who have been where you want to go, ask one close male and one close female friend who knows the most about where you want to go. Ask them the same questions you would have asked the two people who had traveled there.

The reason to talk to people who share your values is so they can help you stick to your boundaries while you are on vacation when your personal and professional support team aren't with you.

The reason for choosing a close man and a close woman friend who have been where you want to travel is because people in different cities and states think differently. For example, if you plan on going to Salt Lake, Utah, you need to know that most people in Utah share a certain religious value. Why is this important to know? To prevent you from embarrassing yourself by making inappropriate jokes or comments about that religion! If you make disparaging remarks about that religion in that city, most of the people there will be irritated with you.

No matter where I go, I would want to know from both men and women:

- What is the crime rate?
- What is the crime rate against women and children?
- What are the most common crimes?
- Are the people there friendly or do they keep to themselves?
- What's the weather like?
- What kind of clothes should I pack?

Set up a time to talk to your support team. However, take into account that if you want something from them, it would be wise to meet with them anytime that's convenient for them.

You should be able to say everything you want to, nicely without your support team interrupting you. Whether or not your support team is quiet the whole time you are talking, you should give them the *respect* you wish to have! Be quiet and listen to them until they are done telling you their concerns! Even if they talk when you are talking, <u>*don't*</u> talk when it's their turn.

Tell your support team everything you know about where you want to travel and what you have learned. These could be things like:

- Ways to stay healthy (i.e., everything related to medication, etc.).
- How you are going to stay safe?
- Tell them who you talked to and why if you need to.
- Tell them how much money you have for the trip.
- Tell them how much money you have budgeted for food, hotel, transportation, emergencies, etc.

Letting them know that you will call is a smart idea. (This shows that you care about how they feel.) Be honest with them! After both of you have heard everything each other has to say, then have a question and answer time.

TO SUPPORT TEAM: Let the choice maker tell you what they know and have learned about where they want to travel. Tell them your personal experiences such as if/when you had to travel out of town for your job, vacation, and/or for emergency reasons. Tell them any difficulties you had regarding traveling. For example, if there's a family emergency, if you have a job, you have to explain to your boss what has happened, take any extra money that you were saving and spend it where you didn't plan to.

Also, if you, as part of the support team, still have things that concern you, tell them. Ask them any question you have so they won't be as worried. Let the choice maker give you all the answers they currently have and allow them as much time as they might need to look up the answers to your questions for themselves and to see if they can answer your questions to be more independent instead of having you tell them they can't do something.

All the money questions in this chapter should help the

person who wants to travel to know if they can afford to travel without being told 'it's too expensive' or 'they can't afford it.'

Let them find the answers for themselves whether that is through the internet, over the telephone, or asking anyone they choose to ask. They may ask their best friend, a brother/sister, a rabbi/pastor, or you; however, who they ask should be their choice.

Waiting until they ask you for help builds up their independence. Therefore, help them only when they ask for your help. Independence in this sentence means how much information they can find on their own and how much a person can look up or do before needing help. This includes knowing when to ask, what questions to ask and who to ask.

TO THE BOTH OF YOU: *<u>Let them be as independent as you think is healthy!</u>*

Chapter 16

Protecting Yourself in General

Here is a list of terms for this chapter. Read through what these words mean two or three times before you continue reading! It is very important to understand these words!

"Knowledge" is facts. Facts = knowledge.

"Understanding" is knowing why you make your decision(s).

"Experience" means things you do regularly that will help you make choices in the future.

"Good choices" are healthy choice(s) made without experience.

"Wise choices" are healthy choice(s) made with experience and knowledge.

When you get educated about something before making a choice, you are making an informed choice!

Through my job, I learned how to ask the right questions to get the answers I needed from businesses before I made my decision. How? My job was doing telephone surveys.

"Right choice" means doing things that are smart, healthy and safe.

There are "foolish choices," "bad choices," and "wrong choices." Sometimes, it is okay to make a foolish, bad, or even a wrong choice depending on what it is! Why? If you never make a foolish, bad, or wrong choice, you will *never* learn from those mistakes. The goal is to *learn* from your mistakes and don't keep making the same mistake(s). There are some mistakes society won't let people make because the risk is too dangerous to your or someone else's health or safety!!

The only way I agree with the intellectually disabled population making any foolish, bad, or wrong choices is after they have been *informed* three times in three different ways. If they still want to make foolish, bad, or wrong choices, then that's on them.

"Informed consent" or informed choice is when someone lets you know what could or will happen if you make that choice. Informing someone can be done in writing. For example, I signed a two-year contract that said, "If I break this contract, I will have to pay them $200." Another example of informed consent is educating a child about their responsibilities if the parent buys them a pet.

<u>With all the information people gather from every possible source, people are informed!</u> Hopefully, the information will help them make better choices.

"Foolish" means lacking the knowledge and experience to make a smart choice. A person could lack knowledge if they are young. Anybody who ignores the advice of someone who has more knowledge than them is foolish! Everyone starts out with *no* experience. However, each time you do something, you gain experience.

If the person *got the information explained to them in three different ways and keeps insisting on doing it their way*, then let them do it. The choice maker should be held legally responsible, *not* the support team. The person should get the credit for the good or bad choices **they** make! And they need to learn to take responsibility for their choices—good and bad!

"Bad choice" is a choice that was made because you didn't know what would happen. Either you didn't know or you were *still learning*. A bad choice could be the choice to smoke even though you know it stinks, but you also have friends that smoke. It would be a bad and/or foolish choice if joining your friends is the *only* reason you started. (If friends make bad choices and you go along never looking at other information, your choice is foolish.)

"Wrong choices" are things that are against the law or things that put someone else in a very unhealthy and/or very unsafe situation. For example, I would do everything I could to stop my family and friends from taking *illegal* drugs because it is dangerous!

Giving your bank account and social security number to people over the phone or over the computer is very unsafe and bad because it can hurt you financially. It puts your money in danger of being stolen electronically, and that's what makes it <u>*wrong*</u>! A person who gives their social security number and/or their bank account number to a person who is not at work has a higher risk of having their money stolen!

Even if you start out making poor choices you *can* learn to make better choices. Ask your support team to help you make better choices and to understand the consequences of different choices, so you will make better choices. *You* should be the one choosing who you want to be part of your team. This team would be the ones to help you see things in different ways, but they should allow you to make up your own mind unless you want them to make a choice for you!

The ideas in the rest of this chapter come from a couple of different people. I use most of these ideas to protect myself. However, the ideas I don't use are still good ideas! Choices could depend on your lifestyle as a whole and/or your ability to pay for it. For example, because of my lifestyle, I should have a cell phone at all times because I stay out until it is dark and I ride the disability van by myself.

For health and/or safety reasons, you should have a cell phone if you:

- Get home after dark
- Have health problems
- Are out in public alone
- Have children
- Easily get lost

The next part is written for the people who want to live in an adult family home, group home, etc., but who also want to go into the community for the day without a caregiver. These people just want their caregivers 'at the house!' At other times, the resident may want a caregiver with them in the community.

(The problem I have noticed is the support team forces people to receive services/things that they do not want or would like to learn to live without!) When it's possible, go out in a group of two or more because there's safety in numbers, but it is not always possible.

What to say when you meet someone new:

- Greet them by saying, "Hi."
- Make "small talk" with new people.
- Check their body language.
- Did they smile, or look away, or down?
- Did they say anything to you?
- If so, what did they say?
- You have to decide from what they say and their body language if they want to continue talking or not.

If they want to talk, here are some safe topics to talk about until you get to know each other better. You can talk about the place where you met, sports, weather, music, news, food, college, or employment.

How long you have known someone, where you know them from, who the friend is, and who's around will depend on subjects. Get the other person to talk about a subject and then share your thoughts about the same subject.

*Don't try to get to know everything about everybody and no one should try to get to know everything about you.

Here are some unsafe topics (at least at first): When you first meet someone, religion and politics should be off limits. You can choose to bring up the subjects after getting to know the other person a little bit. The exception would be if you meet at a religious or political function or organization. If that's where you met them, then those subjects should be okay to talk about.

Other unsafe topics:

If there is a subject that bothers you or the other person, don't talk about that subject to that person. It may rub you or them the wrong way.

Here is an example: I get irritated with the door-to-door style of giving a religious message because I'm happy with my faith; however, I like to *know* what other people's faith is and watch *their faith* in action. So, if I'm <u>*ever upset*</u> with my religion, I can watch them and see if their lives are better and happier, or see how *their faith* pulls them through the challenges of life—if and how *their faith* keeps them going. This kind of research is how I make some of my choices.

Right now, <u>*I am happy with my faith*</u>. I don't want people at my door telling me I will be happier with a different religion! I also don't want salespeople at my door! I don't need the new services or new products that door-to-door salespeople are selling. When it comes to buying something, I want to shop around for it myself! I need my home to be peaceful and safe from door-to-door missionaries and salespeople. I have nothing against people of other religions or salespeople as long as that's not their reason for knocking on my door! If I buy what salespeople want me to buy, I won't have enough money to buy the things I need or want. That's why I don't want them knocking on my door or in my home! By keeping quiet about things that one person has a strong opinion about, it lowers the irritation level!

Neither one of you should be sharing each other's problems because it can lead to advice giving or asking for advice. These people are not part of your "support team." Neither one of you know each other well enough to give each other advice. The only people who should give you advice is your professional and personal support team!

- Never make personal remarks about someone's looks.
- Never gossip.
- Never lie about anybody.
- Never complain.
- Never flirt with people you don't know!

Get to know them before choosing if they are safe unless you are in extreme danger!

*It is wrong to ask or be asked, how much money do you make, when do you get paid, and what day of the week do you get paid? If you answer any of these questions honestly, you make it very easy for people to take financial advantage of you. If you tell someone the answers to these money questions, they might ask you for money on payday or you put yourself in more danger of someone stealing your money or your paycheck. If you give them your bank account number, they could take money out of your account electronically and you would not know it until it's too late!

Unsafe Behaviors

- Borrowing or lending money or things of high personal or dollar value.
- Accepting rides from strangers.
- Accepting or asking for favors from strangers.

TO BE SAFE:
- Know your surroundings.
- Walk with your head up and shoulder's back.
- Walk as if you know where you are going.
- Walk like you must get somewhere!
- *Never* show fear.
- Stay true to your boundaries!

Set *your* boundaries with the help of your support team. You choose who you want on your professional and personal support team. Trust them to protect you if and when your boundaries are violated! Trust them to help you enforce your boundaries, so it will be difficult for anyone to break them!

Tell them what your boundaries are and why those are *your*

boundaries, especially if your support team disagrees with your boundaries for "health or safety reasons." You may need or want to explain your reason(s) for your choice(s). You can ask them to help you set some of your boundaries if you struggle with setting them or enforcing consequences.

Who you choose to be around can protect you or put you in danger. Everyone needs to protect their health! Depending on the kind of person you are, or want to be, people may see you as a safe or a dangerous person. People may see you as a person to be friends with or to avoid. For the first three years, it may be a smart idea to have your support team help you to know who is safe, unsafe, or neutral.

*_Use caution at all times_: If anyone is physically bothering you in the community, here are four more things you can do to protect yourself:

- Take a self-defense class.

Someone _who_ wants to hurt you doesn't care if you have a disability, but you need to use your abilities and work around your disabilities to protect yourself if you are being attacked!

- Get a cell phone even if it's only for emergencies!

There is one kind of phone call that the state and federal government says is free! The free phone call is for health and safety reasons. Ask your support team if having a cell phone would help you be healthier and safer. If you have a cell phone, would your support team feel more comfortable with you living on your own or going out in public by yourself?

- If someone is bothering you and you call the police.

The officer needs to know _who_ is bothering you. They need to know what the person looks like. They will want to know their gender, eye and hair color, and any identifying marks like tattoos, freckles, etc. They will ask you for their name and any of their personal information you know like their address, e-mail address, phone number, etc. They will also want to know if you know the suspect. They will want your name, phone number, address, and e-mail address so the investigator can contact you.

- Get one or more of these items: mace, pepper spray, or a zapper.

You only use them when you need to stop someone from physically or sexually hurting you!! Never use the above items when you are not in immediate danger! I personally don't use a whistle because it is also a child's toy. I only want to use something that is used to signal for help. If I need help, I don't want there to be a mistake. I want someone to help me when I need it!!

Know the time and where your disability van or city bus will pick you up, especially in public!

If you live by yourself or have a roommate(s): You are responsible for yourself and they are responsible for themselves.

*These are ways of protecting your home:

- Keep your doors and windows closed and locked when you leave.

Anyone can walk through the door! Anyone can tear off a screen from a window; however, it slows them down! This is why your windows should be closed and locked, especially at night!

- *Never* go to sleep with the doors or windows open or unlocked at night!

Chances are they will walk into your home or tear the screen off your window if you leave something unlocked. Again, locking them slows them down!

- Put timers on your lights so lights turn on and off in different rooms to make it look like you are home even when you are not home!

Here's an example. The lights are on in the kitchen, and then get turned off in 45 minutes. A minute later the living room lights turn on. You program the lights to be turned on and off in the same way you would do it when you are really home.

How long does it take you to walk from one room to the next room? That answer is the amount of time it takes you to turn the light off in one room and the light on in the next room is how you program it. *It's about the safety of your home when you are gone.* This is to make people think you are home even when you are not! If you own or are buying your home, you can get a security system.

Chapter 17

Money Wise

All government social service workers who ask you for your social security number and/or bank information need it, but you might need or want someone from your support team with you until you learn how to double-check that someone really is who they say they are! If they prove that they really do work for a social service organization, give them all the information they ask for.

Make them prove they work there! Here's how to positively know they are who they say they are:

1) Make them show you their name tag. It will show the name of the company they work for.
2) If you are not sure, call the company and ask them if they have an employee by the name that's on the name tag.
3) If you have never met someone who is coming to your home, find out from their company their name and what they look like. (If you've never met them, you may want to call the company just to make sure this person really works for the company.)

Things to look out for financially:

- A social service agency will *never* ask you for social security number or bank information over the internet.
- They will usually have you bring information into the office or they will come to your house if they need *any* information, *especially financial.*
- Social service agencies can do interviews over the phone.
- Social service workers will tell you in advance before they send something in the mail for you to sign.

If you get something in the mail from your social service agency that only wants you to sign your name at the bottom and no one from the agency told you they were sending it, _call them to find out if they sent you the letter_! If they didn't, **don't sign it and shred the paper**!

- Face-to-face contact is best when doing business that involves signing a contract and sharing private financial information, including using your debit or credit card number, but not always practical.

If you can't buy something in person, then buying it over the phone is the next best choice. If buying online is the only way to buy something, I'd give my money to someone on my support team to buy it and have them give it to me.

- Never ever give your social security number, your credit card and/or debit card number to anyone who is not at work!
- Communicate with your support team *before* you sign anything!

When you sign something, it is called a contract. You have to sign a contract to:

- Rent an apartment/home
- Buy a car
- Buy a cell phone
- Open a bank account

*Contracts are legally binding! Signing a contract shows that you agree to everything that is written on the paper you signed. If you don't understand something, ask _before_ you sign it. If you need to, ask if you can take it with you. Show it to your support team and if the support team says it's okay, then sign it.

*KEEP A COPY FOR YOURSELF!

In my opinion, if you buy things with cash, you will have fewer money problems!

Chapter 18

Car Safety Tips

When riding or driving in a vehicle, *lock the doors*! If you keep your doors unlocked, anyone (i.e., a violent stranger) can come up, open the door and do anything they choose to do.

When you are not in the vehicle, lock the door so no one can break in. They may want to steal just the radio, something you bought from the store, the vehicle itself, or they might want to wait for you and hurt you.

*No matter what a thief wants to steal, having your doors locked slows them down!

Chapter 19

Resources in the Community

There are many kinds of resources including books, services, and others. The internet is one of the largest resources. There are many organizations that can be found on the internet that assist various people or needs. For example, if a car breaks down, you find a mechanic (resource) to fix it.

There are also umbrella organizations that help kids, teens, the disabled population, seniors, and more. The kinds of resources that I will be writing about in this chapter will help everybody be more independent.

Before I moved out of my parents' house, my mom got me connected with the Division of Vocational Rehabilitation (DVR). DVR got me in touch with another agency that taught me how to live independently. The agency taught me how to be assertive. Assertive people can tell others their needs and wants in a nice way!

Some people are "passive." "Passive" means rarely or never telling others what you like, love, need, or want. Passive is also keeping your opinions to yourself, and it is going along with the crowd *even when you should speak up*. An example of passive would be never telling others what you like to eat or never telling anyone what restaurant you would like to eat at.

The problem with that is, someone is always making choices for you and when something is extremely important to you, you might not have the ability to say what you need to say! If you never speak up on the smaller issues, how are you going to speak up when something is important such as preventing someone from getting hurt?

Now that I know how to be assertive, I could never be passive when I have a need or a want.

Another example of being assertive is, when I planned my birthday party at a restaurant, I chose where to have it. However,

I listened to my friends' opinions of where they would want to eat before I made the final choice because it was *my* party! I chose a buffet style restaurant, so everyone could choose what they each wanted to eat.

There are also people who are "aggressive." "Aggressive" people tell other people what to do and say. They may even tell them when to do things. Aggressive people are very controlling because they want to get their own way. (If I'm not careful, I can come across as aggressive.) Aggressive people only care about themselves or come across as 'only caring about themselves'!

Finally, there are "passive-aggressive" people. These people are quietly frustrated for a very long time without looking angry on the outside, then suddenly they explode with anger on everyone! This cycle repeats itself over and over until they learn new patterns to break bad habits!

The goal of the agency that taught me these skills was to help people with disabilities learn how to live independently in a way that will help them avoid being a victim. It also teaches them how to get what they need and want without making someone else a victim.

After I moved out of my parents' house, I started learning how to ride the city bus. I wasn't always able to ride when I had to, so I was given paperwork. I filled it out and had my doctor fill out the medical part. Then we had to mail the form to the transportation company and wait. It took them a couple of weeks to decide if I was eligible to ride the disability van. I was eligible, so when I can't ride the city bus, I take the van. I was taught how to schedule my own van rides.

TO THE CHOICE MAKER: IF you can figure out how to travel around every day on the city bus or the disability van without any help, then your support team would be more likely to let you live on your own.

If others in authority see that someone can't or refuses to speak up for himself/herself, that person might need a power of attorney or guardian. This should be seen as the last option. A good power of attorney or guardian will take the time to get to know the person they are speaking on behalf of!! A good power of attorney or guardian will also know what the person likes, dislikes, and hates and the reasons or possible reasons they feel that way. If a power of attorney or guardian must make a choice against a choice maker's wishes, they need to at least know how the choice maker thinks things through to make the next best choice!

You need to realize that if you have a power of attorney or guardian as a resource, they have legal requirements they must follow. At this time, their primary legal requirement is to make sure the person is kept healthy and safe.

If you dislike the way(s) in which you are being kept healthy and safe, it's time to fight for what you believe in through the political system. This is done by contacting people who work in the government. You can contact them by making phone calls, writing/e-mailing letters, or going to their office. There are people who work in the county or city you live in. There are people who work for the state and others who serve federally (the country).

Some of *my* weakest skills are meal planning, cooking, and shopping for food. I don't know how to read nutrition facts on the back of labels or follow recipes. I physically have trouble standing on my feet, and I have trouble working with both hands. I have a caregiver that helps me grocery shop, meal plan, read labels (when I ask her to), and cook. I also have trouble with a few personal care tasks.

Here is a short list of what personal care tasks are:

- Help walking
- Help taking a shower
- Help to get and take medication(s)
- Help getting dressed
- Help someone transfer from bed to chair, etc.
- Help with teeth, hair, etc.

Everyone needs help at some time and in different ways! To

get a caregiver, a caseworker must approve it and tell the caregiver what they can and can't do!

One agency tried to teach me all the skills related to cooking and keeping a house. However, I still had trouble physically cooking and cleaning house and remembering to wear gloves when cleaning so I was given a caregiver to do what I could not. I did learn some tasks, but I always got very tired after doing some of the chores, so even though I knew how to do the tasks mentally, physically I couldn't do anything for two days after doing some chores, so I was given a caregiver. <u>*I gladly accepted the help!*</u>

It takes a long time to budget money well enough in order for those who care about you not to worry about you financially. Nobody learns how to manage money good in a day or a week. Smart people get advice from their support team. They might read books, take classes, or get information from the internet.

<u>*It takes learning, discipline, and practice to manage money correctly!*</u>

*IF you have trouble budgeting, you can get a representative protective payee (a resource). The payee will make sure *all* of your required and optional bills are paid before you get your spending money. The payee will work with each client, their money, and their schedule to choose when the client should come and get their money. The payee may give the client their money one day of the week, like every Thursday, or the payee may give them spending money two times a month (like getting paid every two weeks), or a payee might give them all their money at one time for the month.

If I had trouble budgeting money, here are a few reasons I would **want** a payee *at first*! I'd want to learn to manage my own money as soon as possible <u>*if that's possible*</u>. Why?

- Having a payee costs money.
- A payee is another bill.

However, it is better to have an extra bill and have someone manage my money, so I don't go into debt and lose everything I own. I would want to learn to manage my money as soon as possible so I could have one less bill. That way, every month, I could save or spend that extra money on something I want.

If someone fails to pay bills, they will lose whatever does not get paid. Examples of this would be having the phone, electricity, or cable shut off. Unpaid bills will result in services getting shut off or products getting taken away. If this happens, that person will have bad credit!

A problem I'd have if I had a payee is that I could only get my money at certain times, so if I wanted to buy something on sale, I couldn't get the money out even if it is a good deal for me because it's not my scheduled day to get money. By managing my own money, I can go to the bank and get the money to buy what's on sale. I can also use a debit card.

To help me or anyone else live as independently as possible, caseworkers can and will help their client's get assistive technology devices. Assistive technology devices can help people who have disabilities do more for themselves. Examples of assistive devices would be, button hooks, easy open medication bottles (which allow people with no use or very little use of their hands to dress themselves and take their own medications), etc. All in all, that agency taught me or tried to teach me how to live healthy.

Safely cooking is for everyone's safety. For example, if you don't turn the stove off when you're done cooking, your house or neighborhood could burn down.

If you rarely eat healthy food, your health is in danger! (If you are physically challenged or are attracted to food, it is to your benefit to ask for help with grocery shopping. This help could come from family, friends and/or caregivers.)

Keeping yourself clean is as important as keeping your house clean. This keeps germs from forming on your body which will prevent you from getting sick. (This helps your physical health!) It is also important to stay clean because if you look dirty and smell bad, people will treat you bad. By keeping yourself clean, you might be protecting yourself from being teased.

Keeping your house clean is for everyone's safety and health because if your house gets too messy, your papers might get on the heaters or stove in the kitchen and catch your house on fire, and a fire can spread to other homes.

There are different safety and health problems when the dishes are constantly dirty, the floors are rarely swept, or when the bathrooms or bedrooms are rarely dusted or vacuumed. A house can be mildly cluttered with papers and clothes, but never cluttered with food! The reason food can never be part of the clutter on the floor is, ants and other bugs are attracted to it and that's not sanitary. My parents would put food on the floor long enough for the cat to eat the leftovers, then they picked it up so ants and other bugs would stay out of the house.

Advocating for yourself protects you from being "taken advantage of." System advocacy is when many agencies help people who have many different kinds of disabilities stand together to protect everybody's services and rights so they can continue to live like everyone else does! After all, if we, as the disabled community, lose our cash benefits, food-stamps, medical benefits, job coaches, transportation, etc., how would we survive?

Tell only the professionals who need to know about your money. This would be so businesspeople can find out if you can pay for something every month such as a cell phone, a house, a car, etc. Another group of people who need to know your private information are those who help you apply for any kind of assistance.

You *need* to know *all* of your rights and responsibilities <u>*before you sign anything*</u>! If you tell your friends and family how much money you make, they might want you to give it or loan it to them. They might not pay you back. You will be kept financially safer in a couple of ways if friends and family don't know how much money you have. Don't give your financial information to anyone who does not need to know.

- First, no one knows if you have money. The fewer people who know, the fewer people will try to rob you.
- Second, fewer people will ask you for your money because they will think you have no money.
- Third, even when you do have money "on you," you still can't afford to hand out money if no one is paying you back! <u>You can use your money just as much as anyone else!</u>
- Fourth, strong recommendation: Don't loan people money! Loaning money is what banks/credit unions are for!!

I tried to cover as many subjects as possible in this book, but none of them in very much detail. It is up to you to find out what your needs and wants are. My goal has been to provide you with a little information and questions in every chapter so you can make educated decisions about how you *live your life*!

Most authors who write self-help books usually focus on one subject such as losing weight or managing money, and they usually go into detail on how to do whatever subject they chose to write about. No matter what the subject is, it's smart to ask different people *you trust* for their help and opinions.

Chapter 20

Is Guardianship Good or Bad and Do You Need or Want One?

**Anybody can get an:

- Advanced directive (medical and mental health)
- Living will
- Will
- Durable power of attorney (DPOA) and/or a power of attorney (POA) as long as a guardianship process has not been established!

An advanced directive, an advocate, a DPOA, a POA, a trustee, a will, and a living will *are all less restrictive options* to stay in control of your choices if **you lose the ability to make **your own** choices. (If you are dissatisfied with who is making your decisions or if you are upset about the decisions they make, talk to a lawyer.)

Take reasonable health precautions! Take responsibility for your own actions!

"Surrogate decision-maker" in this book means someone who makes the choices that a person needs and wants made when he/she can't. The surrogate decision-maker can make choices for the incapacitated/incompetent person because they talked to each other about their wishes before they became incapacitated and/or incompetent.

"Guardianship" is a legal process to see if someone needs a guardian. The process of guardianship is done in court. It is a smart idea (in my opinion) for the judge or jury to see who they are making a decision about.

As I teach you what some of the words or phrases mean, I will also take you through the legal process using easier language.

This information is to be **used as a guide**! If you have *specific questions* or an open legal case, talk to a lawyer! If you don't have a lawyer, get one!

"Representative" means someone who stands up for other people. *Each state has different guardianship laws. If you need to know the guardianship laws, ask a lawyer.

Since most people hate other people having *all* of the control over their lives, a judge or jury will *try to find* the least amount of control! They will use the phrase "Least Restrictive Alternative."

"Least Restrictive Alternative" means the judge or jury will look at all other options such as a representative protective payee, advocate, a trustee, or power of attorney before appointing a guardian. A guardian is the ***last option***!

A judge or jury will make a legal decision in Superior Court when someone applies to be a guardian or when a decision needs to be made about an individual needing an extra layer of protection. To the best of my understanding, the guardianship process gets started when someone applies to be a guardian over someone else. A guardian ad litem is assigned by the court.

Here's what some of the above words or phrases mean:

"Proposed" – When the word "proposed" is used *before* the words guardian, ward, protected person, or vulnerable person, "proposed" means the court has not made a decision yet!

Two other ways of saying 'proposed ward' would be proposed protected person or proposed vulnerable person. ("Ward" and "ward of the state" are legal terms.)

"Guardian ad litem" (GAL) – A guardian ad litem is a lawyer appointed by Superior Court. A GAL's job is to find out what is in the best interest of the proposed person. The GAL must get medical/mental health, behavioral, educational (IQ) records, and find out what the goals, likes/dislikes, etc. are of the individual. The GAL *must* talk to everyone involved in the protected person's life which include the proposed protected person, their caregiver's, the proposed guardian, close and extended family that have an interest in them, their friends and clergy (if applicable), etc. After looking at the overall safety and health of a person and doing all the interviews, the GAL's final job is to write a report to the judge or jury of what they think would be the safest and least restrictive alternative before any kind of guardianship is considered! Sources: Guardianship Services of Seattle and National Guardianship Association Inc.

A GAL is a lawyer who is not required to have human services skills. It is rare to find a GAL who has human services skills. If you know anything based on facts, only report it to the GAL. Sources: Guardianship Services of Seattle and National Guardianship Association Inc.

"Interested person" means anyone in the community who has a concern for the proposed protected person or protected person. Interested people need to make their concern(s) known based only on facts! Make any concerns known to the GAL.

If there's a specific problem, tell the GAL the date(s) of the specific problem, what happened at the time, and the results. They need to know every time this happens, what were the circumstances, and how long the problem has gone on. This helps the GAL keep everything straight in their head so the report(s) make sense to the judge or jury reading the report!

It would be very smart to go to their hearing! If it's your hearing, tell them that you want certain people at your hearing. During the hearing, the judge or jury will make a decision about how competent/capacitated the proposed protected person is.

"Competence/competent person" means a person's thinking ability. How do they solve problems, make choices, and get things done? Competence is referring to a person's thinking ability to make judgments and choices!

"Incompetence/incompetent person" means the lack of ability to make choices, and/or not mentally follow through.

"Capacitated/capacitated person" is a legal term for a person who is physically able to take care of himself/herself. The judge or jury might not give them a guardian, but might look into assigning them an advocate, payee, trustee, etc. to assist them.

"Incapacitated/incapacitated person" is a legal term for a person who is physically unable to take care of themselves. If a judge or jury decides that a proposed protected person is incapacitated, the person will get a guardian if there is no other resource that will successfully help them.

At the end of a hearing the judge or jury will decide if a person is:

- Competent or incompetent
- Capacitated or incapacitated

"Protected person" means the judge or jury has decided that a person is "incompetent" and/or "incapacitated," so the word "proposed" gets dropped. When that decision has been made, they are a "protected person."

"Limited guardian" is a guardian that has partial control. There are many kinds of limited guardians. Contact a lawyer or your state capitol to find out what all the types of guardians are in your state. Each state is different.

There are two types of common limited guardians:

- Guardian of the person
- Guardian of the estate

"Guardian of the person" means having power over the protected person; "person" meaning protecting their body medically and protecting them from abuse. How? The guardian of the person is in charge of talking to all the doctors, caregivers, pharmacies, etc. and is responsible for making sure _all_ the medical professionals work together! I don't know how they protect them from abuse because they are also there to protect them from anyone who has hurt them in the past and to prevent them from getting hurt. I don't know if they have any other jobs. If they do, I don't know what they are!

"Guardian of the estate" has control over large amounts of assets such as a house, car, truck, camper, property, stocks, bonds, cash, etc. A lawyer (including a free lawyer) can help the protected person know what they can do and what the guardian's job is. There are a couple of other choices related to having control over a protected person's assets.

Other choices are a:

- Trustee
- Representative protective payee
- Financial power of attorney

"Bond" protects the individual's money and any other things of high value (i.e., car, house, and things that are expensive).

"Full guardian" has 100% responsibility for the protected person and that includes the requirement of talking to the protected person, but they need to get the person's opinion. However, the guardian is 100% responsible for everything that happens to them.

If the guardian goes on a vacation, gets sick, is temporarily incapacitated, or dies, the standby guardian temporarily fills in. They can apply to be the new appointed guardian if the original guardian is no longer able to be a guardian.

Anyone can apply to be a guardian, but the judge or jury will usually consider a family member or the standby guardian first.

"Standby guardian" becomes legally responsible when the guardian is *not able to do the job*! It is illegal and wrong for guardians to make choices for them *based on the guardian's beliefs*. The guardian must make decisions based on the individual's values, beliefs, goals, desires, needs, wants, etc.

The job requirements to be a guardian:

- Must be at least 18 years old
- Live in the same state as the protected person
- Have a sound mind
- Never have been convicted of a felony

In Washington State, on a legislative level, guardians are given two guidelines in the process of decision-making:

- "Substituted judgment"

- Looking out for the individual's "best interest!"

"Substituted judgment" occurs when a guardian finds out how the person made choices before the individual became incompetent/incapacitated. The guardian must look at their overall lifestyle including their social, religious, political, multicultural, and economic background. They must look at <u>*everything*</u> *that is important* <u>*to them*</u>!

"The principle of substituted judgment is considered to be the manner in which the autonomy, values, beliefs, and preferences of the protected person are best protected." Source: National Guardianship Inc.

On the other hand, if a GAL is unable to find out anything about their values, goals, wants, desires, etc. or how they would make choices, then the GAL will use the second guideline. This is called looking out for their "best interest."

At the time, my only understanding of guardianship was when a guardian makes medical and mental health choices on behalf of a protected person so their medical condition stays the same or gets better. However, everyone should take care of their own health, whether they are disabled or not. Being healthy cost less taxpayer dollars.

In order for a guardian to make choices that would be closest to the protected person's personal choices, the guardian must learn as much as possible about the person they are representing so they will be able to respect their wishes with the exception of anything that puts the individual's health or safety in danger. Health and safety are most people's two most important issues.

Guardians may have to get advice from medical and financial professionals or from "special ethics committees" in order to act in the best interest of their protected person.

My *personal* opinion is that having a guardian is an excellent idea for health and medical reasons. <u>*If you think*</u> healthcare professionals misunderstand and/or ignore you. If I thought any of my healthcare professionals were ignoring or misunderstanding me, I would get a medical power of attorney or guardian to talk to them for me! Guardians can be great when advocating for a second doctor's opinion when or if there is a disagreement over what to do and they CAN force *all* your doctors to work together!

I saw a situation where a woman could talk, and she had no power of attorney and no guardian! She talked to her medical doctor, mental health professional, care giving agency, and caseworker who were ***all ignoring her*. The healthcare professionals were not working together to meet her needs, physically and emotionally. The result: She died!

If she had had a power of attorney or a guardian for medical and health reasons, ALL her healthcare professionals would have been *legally answerable* to her power of attorney or guardian when she was being misunderstood or was being ignored by her healthcare professionals!

Current laws in some states give guardians the right to choose where the protected person lives. In my opinion, a guardian needs to include the protected person's opinion, but the guardian must have the final say on healthcare issues when their choice is going to put their health in danger. A person must be living in what most people would consider 'safe housing' in order to choose where they live. The guardian should suggest housing options around their health and the protected person can let the guardian know if they have any desires about their housing.

My personal choice was renting an apartment and having a caregiver come into my home for the first ten years. I lived alone, needed and wanted help. A couple of times I ended up in the hospital and then I got more caregiving hours. I chose to take *fewer* hours than my caseworker said I needed. I took what I needed! Each client has a different number of hours that they are eligible for. It is based on an individual's needs!

I talked to a lot of people who have guardians and about half of the protected people who can talk told me they dislike most of the choices their guardian makes. Almost all of the protected people who are unable to talk like their guardian's choices or they don't care what choices they make. (I assume they like the choices that are being made since they can't say if they don't!)

I have seen other responsibilities given to guardians other than for medical and healthcare reasons.

Basically, a protected person must get permission from their guardian before getting married or getting a divorce, vote, or getting a driver's license. A protected person might also have to ask permission to make or revoke a will (or possibly any other kind of legal papers like a living will), to sue someone, to buy, sell, or own property. Finally, a protected person may need to get permission to choose who their friends are. The above statements are *possibly* state law. *All 50 states have different laws!* I'm aware of some of Washington State's laws.

Some protected people I have met want to:

- Choose where they live
- Get married
- Get a cell phone
- Go on a vacation

To my understanding the following doesn't fall under the guardianship laws; however, it may fall within everyday communication skills! (If something requires a financial contract, it might be a guardianship issue!)

In order to be more independent, a protected person should:

- Develop communication skills.
- Re-read the chapters in this book that can help them gain more independence.
- Communicate to and with your support team about everything you would like to do yourself or learn to do for yourself!

"If a person does not have the ability to exercise a right, the person does not benefit by having that right!" (J. Eli Harvey)

If you are interested, look up the state laws for guardianship in your state.

Warning! The GAL's job is a legal job. Many problems arise because the GAL is not required to have any human services skills! They depend on everyone who knows and cares about the protected person to educate the GAL about that individual.

Mismatching a protected person with a guardian who ignores or misunderstands the protected person is extremely unfortunate and unfair to the individual the choices are made for!!

Guardian ad litem must consider all the medical reports but should also include the proposed protected person's strengths! However, an appointed guardian should rarely look at the weaknesses of a protected person. Except for medical and health choices, a guardian should always be looking for ways to help them need less help!

Even when the protected person is in agreement with having a guardian, I have witnessed that older protected people want more freedom.

These freedoms could include:

- What type of job they have
- Where they attend college (for credit or not)
- Which kind of transportation they use
- Getting married or not
- To have children or not

All of these wants requires social/interpersonal skills!

You talk to your employer, family, friends, co-workers, guardian, and strangers in different ways. You need to learn how to speak to different people who have different roles in your life. If you don't know how, ask your support team!

My suggestion would be to see where people are at "maturity-wise" by asking different questions. You gain maturity every day by the choices you make and your experiences.

Questions to ask regarding guardians are:

- Am I the best person to serve as a guardian for the protected person?

- Is this guardian still the right person to serve as the guardian?
- Is there a need for a new guardian?
- Has the protected person learned some things so that the guardian can become less restrictive?
- Has the protected person learned enough skills to become guardian free?

Add in your own questions such as: Does the guardian and the protected person have a personality conflict? Tell the GAL anything you think they should know when making a choice about the best match for the two.

Personally, if I thought someone could do more for himself/herself and I was the judge or on the jury, I would temporarily give the protected person one or two new responsibilities and see what kind of choices they make and how they handle their new freedom. I would want to know if they are learning or need a longer trial. A court appointed guardian would check in on them so they can report back to me in a month. In one month, I'd make the final decision if he/she could keep those freedoms or if the guardian needs to take over again! Then if the protected person would want to, I'd let them try more responsibilities to see how they would manage those responsibilities for one month before I'd make a final choice, etc.

"Guardianship is not the best way to deal with emergencies." www.proguard.org

Legal fees are different depending on which lawyer you go to, but all lawyers do the same work in preventing or establishing a guardian in someone's life!

The person who pays the lawyer would be the proposed protected person, Superior Court, the county, or possibly the guardian. There's a possibility that the cost can be shared among a couple of them. There are legal duties of a guardian that are there to help identify a protected person's needs and to help them access the resources in the community.

A guardian getting a bond is one way to protect the client's money and property. A guardian of the estate can have control over a protected person's government money (and maybe the money they earn at work). If the guardian steals from the protected person, the insurance company pays the money back to the protected person. The guardian must pay the insurance company back and loses the privilege of being a guardian *for life*!

A second way to protect a person's estate is to put a "*block on a bank account*." "A block on a bank account" means having two people watching over the protected person's money, etc. The judge can set boundaries around the guardian. The guardian will need to get permission from the judge before buying some things. A "block on an account" would have to be set up through a bank or a credit union.

The third way of protecting a person's money is by reporting back to court. The judge will require receipts to prove where the money was spent for the person. The guardian has to make financial reports to the judge every 1-3 years to "The Court."

No matter what kind of guardian a protected person has, there are two kinds of legal papers to find out what the protected person is allowed to do and what the guardian must do:

- First, "Letters of Guardianship"
- Second, "Order Appointing Guardian"

Even if a guardian is a full guardian, the guardian can't do whatever they please. The guardian has *no control* regarding if the protected person receives mental health services. If the guardian feels mental health services are necessary and the protected person doesn't want it, there must be a court order.

Guardians have no power over what style of clothes they wear *except* when their choice *endangers their health*! For example, a person can wear a dress, a skirt, leathers, chains, shirts with cigarette ads, Bible, beer, rock stars, or with moral/nice sayings on it! *It is the individual's choice!* There are some clothes that can give you the wrong kind of attention such as being touched by people you don't know.

No matter how you are dressed, no one has the right to touch you without your permission, but some people will break the law and touch others without permission. By dressing modestly, people are *not* as likely to harass you. Ask your support team if you need to understand the health and safety risks of dressing in certain ways.

However, it's illegal and wrong for a guardian to disapprove or approve of *certain* kinds of clothing based on the guardian's values and beliefs. If the guardian tries to tell them what they must or can't wear because of the guardian's values, the protected person has a right to complain to the GAL for two reasons (the guardian's personal values and fears) and not letting the person be separate from the guardian.

The GAL will solve the problem in a way that's fair to everyone. It might be a compromise—both of you might get a little bit of what you want. The GAL might have to take your complaint to their boss. The court is the supervisor over the GAL. The GAL is the guardian's supervisor.

Before anyone makes their decision on the disagreement, the complaint must be researched. Anyone who has any knowledge or facts about the situation has a civil obligation to do or say something, but never based on your personal opinions!

If anyone thinks a guardian and a protected person are *not* the right match for each other or that the establishment of a guardian is no longer needed: Go to a GAL who will mediate or communicate between the guardian and the protected person to find out if the protected person can be responsible for anything new. The protected person might need a different guardian or might not need a guardian at all.

**The GAL will *try* to keep things out of the court and deal with it in the simplest way possible.

**If disagreements can *stay out* of the courtroom, *keep it out* for the *protection* of the *person's identity*!

If anyone thinks there's a problem with the person who is seeking to become the guardian or who became a guardian, report it to the GAL. Report facts such as:

- Specific event(s)
- Dates things happened
- What you saw and heard
- How it affected the protected person

If you disagree with how a GAL handles your concern(s), tell the GAL's supervisor/boss. The (proposed) protected person has a right to a lawyer and you, as an interested person, should attend the hearing.

If you think an established guardian is not meeting the needs/wants of a protected person, there are a couple of ways that I am aware of to deal with your concerns or problems.

First, it is smart to get a lawyer to help you and them through the guardianship process for removal of a guardian.

Second, there is a possibility for seeing if the protected person *needs a less restrictive* kind of guardian and if a judge will allow the person to get *some new freedoms*; with the understanding of them having an advocate/teacher or someone else watching to see if *they know how to stick to their own values*! Basically, they go through the whole legal process with the court again. (It probably has to go through court to prevent taking advantage of someone financially or to make sure their needs are met.)

An interested person can find the guardianship papers in the county courthouse. The papers should be in the office of the clerk. It is best to have the case number, even though the file can be found under the protected person's name.

It is possible for someone who is not a lawyer to stand up for a protected person. However, a lawyer is recommended because the legal papers are very hard to understand. It helps to read the guardianship laws in your state. You can find them in a law library or on the internet.

Guardianship and Intellectually Disabled Individuals

Not all people with disabilities need a guardian. If all the professionals agree that someone with a disability needs a guardian, then the person needs one. If all the professionals agree a person with a disability *doesn't need* a guardian, then the person does not need one, no matter what family and friends say. The reverse is possible—society and the system may think someone needs a guardian and the family may disagree. Either way, the court has the final say!

A judge or jury must agree with the doctor's and/or family member's recommendation that someone needs a guardian. If the judge or jury disagrees, the person won't have a guardian!

WORK WITH ALL YOUR PROFESSIONALS TO GET AS MUCH INDEPENDENCE AS YOU CAN AND/OR WANT!

Understanding Guardianship

Some states offer limited guardianships which allow a protected person to have control over part of their life and the limited guardian to have control over other parts of their life.

One of the roles of any kind of guardian is to include the protected person in making as many choices as they can.

Society believes in "safety and health."

On the other hand, I like adventure, high-risk, independence, and *protecting health*! I understand protecting everyone's health including mine! My high-risk activity is flying in a small airplane—going extra high in the air and nose diving as a co-pilot. (I hate flying in commercial airplanes, but I do fly in them when it's necessary!)

Other high-risk activities could be skydiving, horseback riding, parachuting, etc. (These kinds of high-risk activities don't fall under the "safety and health rules." If you can pay for it and someone tries to stop you, it's a valid complaint!)

If I never did scary things like moving out of my parents' house, getting on a commercial airplane or going to college, I would never have become independent and I wouldn't be as mature as I am.

**GUARDIANS MUST NOT "VIEW" OR "USE" THEIR POSITION TO LIMIT A PERSON'S ACTIVITY!

Chapter 21

Where My Strength Lies

This chapter tells the process of how I came up with my own value system and how you might consider this to be your value system also. It is written for the people who have not set their own value system or want to change their value system.

Faith is a way. However, faith in what or who? Is it a religion? Some people just live by the "Golden Rule," "Treat others the way you want to be treated!" I was raised with very high standards. My parents have extremely high work ethics.

The women in my mom's generation were stay-at-home moms *if* they could afford it! My parents gave money to organizations when they could; however, we always had enough money.

In 10th grade, my first boyfriend invited me to the youth group at his church. The teenagers had more of my parents' morals than the teenagers at my parents' church. Because they were nicer to each other at this church, I finally got the courage to ask my parents if I could go *every* Wednesday night. I later got permission to stop going to their church on Sundays, and started going to *my* church!

You are valuable, <u>even</u> when your choices are different from others! However, it is smart to ask experienced and older people questions before you make a major change.

Even though I was raised in a church and had switched churches, for me church was a social event I chose to go because it was a happy place to be. My *new church* talked about having a personal relationship with Jesus Christ. At first, I did not understand this personal relationship stuff.

With my childhood background, I made a choice to stand back and watch different people in this church and see how they dealt with hard times. I wanted to know what would happen to their faith in Jesus Christ if a family member got really sick or if they found out they had to do something they did not want to do.

It was very interesting *watching* these people to see if what they *said* matched their walk with God when life was going the wrong way. I, by *my choice*, started talking to different people and asking different people questions.

My questions were: "What makes God so real in your life?" "What were you like before you accepted Jesus Christ into your life?" "What are you like today, now that you have a personal relationship with God?" "How long have you had this personal relationship?"

Also, I asked multiple people of various ages who had been Christians for a different amount of years. I got many answers of what is important and what is not, but everyone I talked to had a relationship with Jesus Christ.

Finally, I went to a three-day youth retreat and <u>understood for myself</u> this message of Jesus Christ that my church friends had been trying to explain to me.

I had to ask different people questions <u>before</u> *my ears and heart was opened to understanding <u>what</u>* they said about their faith in Jesus Christ. *This was **my process** of establishing boundaries!*

The difference is knowing that Jesus is in my heart and ruling my heart instead of just knowing the facts in my head and following His commandments by "duty." In March 1988, I went *through the process* of choosing who my value system is based on and I will continue following my value system for the rest of my life.

Having your *own* value system should be *consistent* with what you believe when other people challenge you to do things or not to do things you think is wrong.

Now that I have a *personal relationship with Christ*, I stopped feeling bad for making different choices and I usually don't feel ashamed for making mistakes because I can ask for forgiveness or forgive the other person. When I make mistakes, I can also learn from my mistakes!

How do you make big decisions in life? Is it health? Is it law? Medical reports come out all the time finding new information and laws have been modified or revoked. If these are your standards, what happens when you've been doing something that is unhealthy or becomes unlawful?

If you say it depends on what the law says, remember that our laws could change at any level such as city, county, state, or federal levels. If you make your choices by your religion, then think 'did you chose your religion?'

To me, religious leaders in any religion are just human. They have equal opportunity to make mistakes just like anyone else. **Everyone makes mistakes**!

This is why it is important to have a personal relationship with Jesus Christ. Do you know God personally? He has made a way so we can know Him. He is waiting for you to answer His "call."

You can get forgiveness for **everything** you've ever done wrong in your life. You can also know for sure that you have "everlasting life" through faith/trust in God's only Son, Jesus Christ.

What stops us from knowing God personally? Lack of education of who God is and not knowing what He has done for us!

If you want to know God personally, read on!

(Get a Bible to make sure what is being written here is also what the Bible says.)

Here are some *truths* that will help you find out *how* to meet and know God personally and join in the everlasting life that He promised.

1. GOD LOVES YOU AND MADE YOU TO KNOW HIM PERSONALLY.

GOD'S LOVE

GOD LOVES YOU and He created you to know Him *personally*!

"For God so loved the world that He gave His one and only Son, that whoever believes in Him shall not perish but have eternal life" (John 3:16 NIV). "NIV" means New International Version of the Bible.

GOD'S PLAN
"Now this is eternal life: that they know you, the only true God, and Jesus Christ, whom You have sent" (John 17:3 NIV).

What stops us from knowing God personally? People are *sinful* and *separated* from God, so we cannot know Him personally or experience His love.

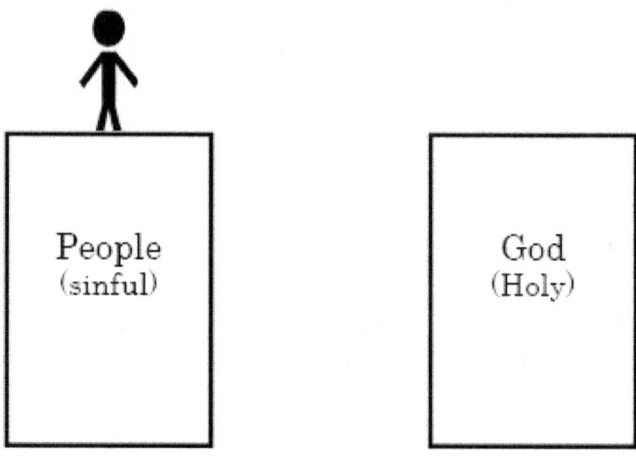

"Sin" is breaking God's laws or "sin" is going against God's laws. Either one of these could happen accidently or on purpose. Even if it is an accident, it's sin!

2A. The next truth is PEOPLE ARE SINFUL.

"for all have sinned and 'fall short' of the glory of God," (Romans 3:23 NIV). "Fall short" or "falling short" means not meeting God's standard of perfection, set by God.

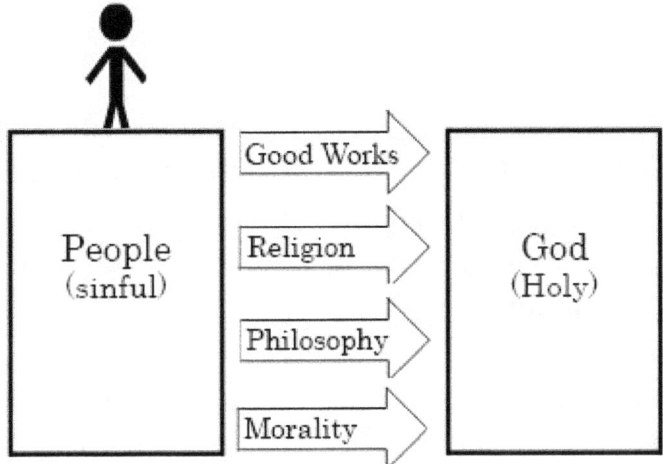

The picture above shows different ways that sinful people try to reach God.

(It is a good idea to volunteer and do good works like go to church at least once a week and live a good life, but not with the purpose of reaching God!)

People were made to have a relationship with God; but because of their own "self-will," they chose to go their own way and break their relationship with God.

"Self-will" means choosing to go your own way and do your own thing. "Self-will" can also be seen when *what* you are doing and saying is for your own "self-pleasure" or if you show a "passive indifference" towards God.

"Passive indifference" means anything goes; you have no opinion (not caring about the things of God, faith, and sin.)

Both doing and saying things that do not make God happy and not caring about the things of God are "evidence of sin."

"Evidence" means facts.

2B. PEOPLE ARE SEPARATED

"For the wages of sin is death..." (Romans 6:23).

The Bible is talking about spiritual separation/death from God. The next truth says the ONLY WAY to reach God is through Jesus Christ.

3. JESUS CHRIST IS GOD'S ONLY WAY TO BRIDGE THE GAP BETWEEN GOD'S PERFECTION AND PEOPLE'S SINFULNESS AND ANY WRONG DOING!

Through Him alone we can know God personally and experience His love.

HE DIED IN OUR PLACE
"But God demonstrates His own love toward us, in that while we were yet sinners, Christ died for us" (Romans 5:8).

HE ROSE FROM THE DEAD
"...Christ died for our sins...He was buried...He was raised on the third day, according to the Scriptures...He appeared to Peter, then to the twelve. After that He appeared to more than five hundred..." (1 Corinthians 15:3-66).

HE IS THE ONLY WAY TO GOD
"Jesus said to him, 'I am the way, the truth, and the life. No one comes to the Father except through Me'" (John 14:6).

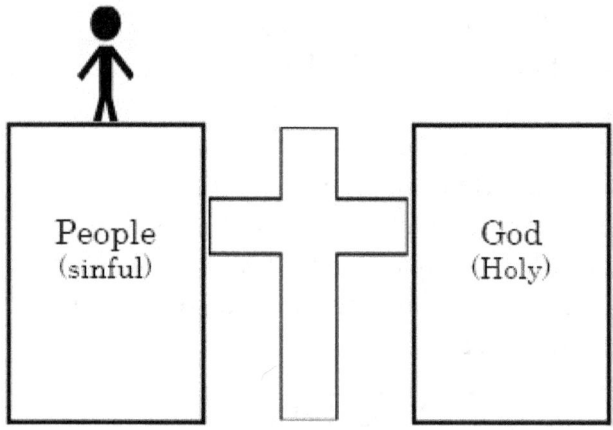

This picture shows how God reached down to sinful people by sending His Son, Jesus Christ to die on the cross in our place to pay the "penalty" for our sins. Penalty means legal punishment for a crime.

It is not just enough to know these facts in your head.

Each person must make "their own choice" to "receive" Jesus Christ as "Savior" and "Lord," then they can know God personally and experience His love.

"Savior" means one who saves. (S with a capital "S," means God.) "Lord" means God having 100% control over people's lives who accept Him as Lord.

THE fourth TRUTH IS YOU MUST CHOOSE FOR YOURSELF TO OR NOT TO RECEIVE JESUS CHRIST INTO YOUR HEART!

"But as many as received Him, to them He gave the right to become children of God, to those who believe in His name" (John 1:12).

"For by grace you have been saved through faith, and that not of yourselves; it is the gift of God, not of works, lest anyone should boast" (Ephesians 2:8-9). Boast means saying proud words. GOD HATES PROUD WORDS!

When we receive Christ, we experience a "new birth." (You can read John 3:1-8.) "New birth" means spiritual birth. We receive Christ <u>by personal invitation</u>.

(Christ is speaking) *"Behold, I stand at the door and knock. If anyone hears My voice and opens the door, I will come in to him..."* (Revelation 3:20). Receiving Christ involves turning to God and away from yourself (by repenting from sin), and trusting Christ to come into your life to forgive you of your sins and make you the kind of person He wants you to be.

It is not enough to only know and accept these facts in your head: That Jesus Christ is the Son of God, and that He died on the cross for our sins (with no heart experience).

It is not enough to only have an emotional experience or good feelings or a heart experience (with no facts).

We receive Christ by faith (into our heart) as an act of the will.

"...if you confess with your mouth the Lord Jesus and believe in your heart that God has raised Him from the dead, you will be saved" (Romans 10:9).

The following two circles represent a "self-centered life" or a "Christ-centered life." Here is what the symbols represent:

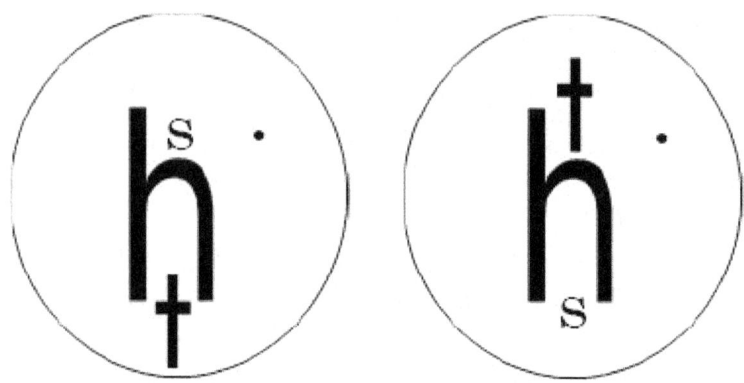

h = throne, s = self, † = Christ, and • = interests directed by who is on the throne.

        Self-directed life   Christ-directed life

Which circle best represents your life?

Which circle would you like to have represent your life?

The following explains how you can invite Jesus Christ into your life.

YOU CAN RECEIVE CHRIST NOW BY FAITH THROUGH PRAYER! (Prayer is talking with God.)

God knows your heart and is not as concerned with your words as He is with the attitude of your heart. The following is a suggested prayer:

"Lord Jesus, I want to know You personally. Thank You for dying on the cross for my sins. I open the door of my life and receive You. Thank You for forgiving my sins and giving me everlasting life. Take control of the throne of my life. Make me the kind of person You want me to be! Amen."

Does this prayer express the desire of your heart or not?

If it does, pray this prayer right now and Christ will come into your heart, as He promised.

HOW TO KNOW THAT JESUS CHRIST IS IN YOUR LIFE

Did you receive Christ into your life? According to His promise in Revelation 3:20, where is Christ right now? Is He inside or outside of you? Christ said that He would come into your life and be your friend, so you can know Him personally.

Would He mislead you? On what authority do you know that God has answered your prayer? (The honesty of God Himself and His Word.)

THE BIBLE PROMISES EVERLASTING LIFE TO ALL WHO RECEIVE CHRIST

"And this is the testimony: that God has given us eternal life, and this life is in His Son. He who has the Son has life; he who does not have the Son of God does not have life. These things I have written to you who believe in the name of the Son of God, that you may know that you have eternal life..." (1 John 5:11-13).

Thank God often that Christ is in your life and that He will never leave you (Hebrew 13:5). You can know on the basis of the promise that Christ lives in you and that you have everlasting life, from the very moment you invite Him in. He will not deceive you.

An important reminder...DO NOT DEPEND ON FEELINGS.

The promise of God's Word, the Bible—not our feelings—is our authority. The Christian life is lived by faith (trust) in God Himself and His Word.

This picture of a train shows the relationship between FACT (God and His Word); FAITH (our trust in God and His Word); FEELINGS (the result of our faith and obedience). (John 14:21)

The train will run with or without the caboose. However, it is useless to try to pull the caboose. In the same way, we as Christians do not depend on feelings or emotions, but we place our faith (trust) in the honesty of God and the promises of His Word; not solely on head knowledge (fact).

NOW THAT YOU HAVE ENTERED INTO A PERSONAL RELATIONSHIP WITH CHRIST

The moment that you received Christ by faith, as an act of the will, many things happened including the following:

1) Christ came into your life (Revelation 3:20 and Colossians 1:27).
2) Your sins were forgiven (Colossians 1:14).
3) You became a child of God (John 1:12).
4) You received everlasting life (John 5:24).
5) You began the great adventure for which God created you (John 10:10; 2 Corinthians 5:17; and 1 Thessalonians 5:18).

Can you think of anything more wonderful that could happen to you than entering into a personal relationship with Jesus Christ? Would you like to thank God in prayer right now for what He has done for you? By thanking God, you demonstrate your faith.

To enjoy your new relationship with God...spiritual GROWTH results from trusting Jesus Christ. *"...the righteous will live by faith"* (Galatians 3:11).

A life of faith will enable you to trust God increasing with every detail of your life, and to practice the following GROWTH:

- G Go to God in prayer daily (John 15:7).
- R Read God's Word daily (Acts 17:11) beginning with the Gospel of John.
- O Obey God moment by moment (John 14:21).
- W Witness for Christ by your life and words (Matthew 4:19 and John 15:8).
- T Trust God for every detail of your life (Proverbs 3:5).
- H Holy Spirit–Allow Him to control and empower your daily life and witness (Galatians 5:16-17 and Acts 1:8).

FELLOWSHIP IN A GOOD CHURCH

God's Word encourages us to get together with others who believe in Jesus Christ as their Savior and Lord. (Read Hebrews 10:25 with someone else.) Several logs burn brightly together, but put one aside on the cold hearth, and the fire goes out. So, it is with our relationship with other Christians.

If you do not belong to a good church, do not wait to be invited. Take the initiative, call the pastor of a nearby church where Christ is honored and His Word is preached. Start this week and make plans to attend.

Thank you for taking the time to read this! I hope my story helps you to make your own choices in life!

About the Author

Having been born with lots of disabilities, Tiffani struggled with people in authority who thought she was not able to do very much. She has done a lot!

Because of her faith in God and training in self-advocacy, she has depended on God and gained knowledge of government and business to advocate and to protect herself. She wants to pass these lessons on.

Tiffani is married and has two children.

She spent 18 years writing her story before she found a group of writers to help her publish it.

If this has helped you out in any way, contact the author and let her know at responsiblyindependent@yahoo.com

www.ingramcontent.com/pod-product-compliance
Lightning Source LLC
Chambersburg PA
CBHW072006070526
44583CB00015B/1358